The Evolution of the European Union
Problems and Prospects

THE EVOLUTION OF THE EUROPEAN UNION

Problems and Prospects

DR. PHALNEIKIM HAOKIP

AKANSHA PUBLISHING HOUSE
NEW DELHI-110002 (INDIA)

AKANSHA PUBLISHING HOUSE
4649-B/21, Ansari Road
Darya Ganj, New Delhi - 110 002
Ph.: 23263193 / 9811582579 / 09435116718
Fax: 011-23263193
Email: ektabooks@yahoo.com

The Evolution of the European Union: Problems and Prospects

First Published 2009
ISBN 978-81-8370-157-0

PRINTED IN INDIA

Published by Akansha Publishing House, New Delhi and Printed at Aryan Enterprises, Delhi.

To my

beloved family

for their

love and support

Foreword

Europe has long been a centre of cultural and economic achievement. The ancient Greeks and the Romans produced major civilizations, famous for their contributions to philosophy, literature, fine art and government. The renaissance which began in the 14th century was a period of great accomplishment for European artists and architects, and the age of exploration beginning in the 15th century included voyages to the far corners of the world by the Europeans navigators. As a result, a new world lay to the west. Horizons were widening and European was set to become a player on a larger stage. In the 18th century modern forms of industry began to be developed. But in the 20th century much of Europe was ravaged by the two world wars.

After World War II, ended in 1945, Europe was divided into two major political and economic blocs – communist nations in Eastern Europe falling under the then USSR's influence and the non-communist countries in Western Europe under the USA's dominance. Before long, the tension and suspicions engendered by the geographical proximity of the world's two super-powers took the form of cold war, a taste of resolve that was particularly nerve-racking at the dawn of atomic age. However, between 1989 and 1995, the Eastern bloc broke up with the collapse of the USSR.

In order to regain its lost glory as well as to make itself independent of both the then Soviet Union and the United

States' influence and dictate, the six states of Europe, namely, Belgium, France, Germany, Italy, Luxembourg and The Netherlands initiated to form the European Community which later evolved itself into the European Union (EU).

Miss. Phalneikim's book attempts to examine the historical evolution of the EU as an international regional organization. The EU today is the most important commercial power in the world with a share of 21 per cent of the world trade. With the entry of 10 more members from the Eastern and Central Europe in 2004, the EU is gradually becoming a supra-national structure. Its relative success is often projected as a role model for other regional organizations and restructuring even the United Nations Organization. Therefore, the book will go a long way to serve the needs of students and general readers who are involved in the study of regional and international politics.

Prof Lal Dena
Dept. of History
Manipur University

Imphal
18 February, 2008

Preface

The Evolution of the European Union: Problems and Prospects deals with the structural and orgnaisational development of the European Union since its inception till the year 2004. The period witnessed the transition of Europe from war devastated, fragmented nations and a continent which depend on the US for almost everything to that of a unified, formidable economic giants and an upcoming political force whose present can no longer be ignore in international arena. Throughout, the aim has been to examine the various events and developments that led to the evolution of the EU from EC to EU, the uniqueness of its institutions as well as adaptability to the changing economic and political circumstances. As such emphasis is given on the structural, functional, procedural aspects and policy areas of the EU.

I am deeply grateful to all those people who made this book possible. I am extremely thankful to Prof. CSR Murthy, my M.Phil supervisor and to Prof. Lal Dena, my Ph.D. supervisor. The credit of this book goes to them both. I am also deeply grateful to my parents Paodong and Nengvah Haokip, my sister Lhingkhotin and Hoinu for being a constant source of inspiration, to my brothers Onthang and Jangneh, my sisters-in-law Salemkim and Hatneilhing for their encouragement and support in my endeavour, to Chongrolien, Nivedita, Tinneng, Sheeleima, Alina, Kishorechan who help me in my work in one way or the other.

I would like to thank my publisher Mr. M.P. Misra, Akansha Publishing House, New Delhi especially for taking the work of a novice author like me, for publication. I would also like to thank the library staffs of Jawahalal Nehru University, Manipur University, British Council Library & European Delegation Office, New Delhi for their co-operation and assistance in locating matrial.

The responsibility for error remains mine alone.

Dr. PHALNEIKIM HAOKIP

Content

1
INTRODUCTION

The book seeks to examine the structural and policy dimensions of the evolution of the European Union as an international regional organization from 1952 to 2004.

Regionalism is among the most important and popular approaches to international organizations and cooperation. It has attracted much attention in the years following the World War II. The concept has long been closely associated with the evolution of the European Community, and recently with the various economic regional organizations.

The argument in favour of regionalism – as against the universalist approach for organizing international cooperation revolves around a number of important assertions. At the outset it should be made clear that the two are not antithetical. They, in fact, are complementary processes, occurring simultaneously and feeding on each other.

The proponents of the regional approach to peace usually argue that regional integration is a half-way house between international anarchy and world integration. They argue that taking up every aspect from global point of view is not always feasible. And find that the relative cultural, economic, political and geographical affinity within a region lends itself to more effective organization.

The main assumption of this argument is that being a contiguous area, and also having shared ideology, common culture, historical background and even common problems, regional organizations are more suitable platforms for solving problem.

The proponent of globalism, on the other hand argue that despite the appeal of regional argument, the problem of attaining peace can best be faced at global level. They argue that suitability of regionalism depends on the nature of problems to be dealt. Since all the problems are not similar in nature, some are regional but global in impact, while some are too emotive to be solved by regional organizations. They also argue that regional organizations are often built around the great power and instead of eliminating power conflicts or assuring small states of their security, they usually do not constitute anything more than a formalized area of influence.[1]

Both regionalism and globalism have their own utilities. Regional organizations are particularly suitable for cultivation of intensive cooperation among states while global organizations have special advantages for dealing with conflicts among states.[2]

Both region and regionalism are ambiguous terms. There is no precise and accepted definition and conceptual controversy creeps in as to what constitute region. A common sense way of defining region is on the basis of distinct landmasses such as Europe, Africa, Asia and North and South America. However, in international relations, a region or regional organization is not always confined to particular areas only. It may stretch from one end of the world to the other. As such a region is defined as "an area of contiguous countries defined usually by geography or by common cultural heritage, shared political philosophy or mutual economic interest."[3]

A region, thus, has a geographical connotation, usually having commonalities in terms of culture, religion, way of life and historical background.

Regionalism can also be defined in terms of both socio-cultural factors internal and political factors external to the region. Stoessinger defined regionalism as a tendency where "a group of three or more states join together and whose goal is formation of distinct political identity."[4] A regional arrangement or organization denotes the one which is characterized by group of states coming together for pursuit of common goal/goals. It is voluntary in character comprising of a well-defined institutional structure. Joseph Nye's definition of regionalism covers such diverse functional as well as geographical phenomena as EU, NATO, Commonwealth and Caucusing groups in the UN system. As such Nye used regional organization to describe those organizations which are based on (a) formal agreement among governments, (b) possessing diplomatic forum, and (c) assisted by an associated international bureaucracy.[5] These organizations may be single purpose or multipurpose in activity. They are, however, different from the global organizations like the United Nations in that the former restrict membership on the basis of geographical or ideological considerations.

Regionalism in international relations/politics is, thus, an elastic concept defying any hard and fast definitions. It may stem from security or economic reasons or even from the desire of stronger nations to control and direct the policies of smaller nations whether it is done through persuasions or coercion or both.

Thus, a region is not merely a geographical unit as it is very difficult to define; the same may include as many states as possible, directed against a specific enemy or at collective security of an area in general. It may be a short-term or long-term agreement between three or more states varying in consistency and homogeneity. It may be culturally unified like the Arab League or may be as diverse as NATO and Commonwealth of Nations with its democracies and dictatorship along with different religion, language, caste, creed, etc.

There are three types of regional organizations:

1. Regional Defence Organisations such as NATO, Warsaw Pact.
2. Regional Economic Organisations like the European Community, the Council of Mutual Economic Assistance (CMEA), the Latin America Free Trade Area (LAFTA), etc. and
3. Organisations which have general or multipurpose activity, for instance, the Organisation of American States (OAS), Organisation of African Unity (OAU), the Arab League, etc.

The first type of regional organization developed as a response to the post-World War II cold war environment and the shattering of the dream of global collective security. Most of these were established in the 1940s and 1950s and except for the Warsaw Treaty Organisation (WTO), all the other defence organizations such as NATO (1949), Australia-New Zealand-United States (ANZUS, 1952) Pact, South East Asia Treaty Organisation (SEATO, 1954) bound the US – the mobile global power – with the defense systems of non-communist nation states in these regions.

The second type of regional organizations are purely economic in nature. Without the inclusion of high politics, atleast in the beginning. They have limited membership and are functional purpose organizations. This type exemplifies best the functional approach of regional integration that begins with non-political cooperative arrangement and then gradually spillover into political integration with the passage of time. Examples of this type of organization are European Community, now European Union, ASEAN, LAFTA, etc. of which European Community's experience is the most successful.

The third type is the hybrid of the first and the second and are both functional and defence in characters. However, these organizations are not effective enough and often fell prey at the hands of the wider East- West conflicts.

As mentioned earlier regionalism as a form of international cooperation and organization is relatively a post-World War II phenomenon. However, the faith of regionalism was sealed by the East-West tension in which both the superpower vied with each other to enlarge their respective area of influence. During this period, there was a scant regard for regional cooperation and many, with a few exceptions like the EC remained far from effective. After the end of the cold war, regionalism started to gain new importance in international politics. There were global economic changes which led to worldwide effort towards integration of economies. This coincided with the dilution of cold war rivalry because of the efforts of both the superpowers. As such, "newer sets of regional arguments were emerging, which were informed by a consciousness of the geopolitical environment in which they were operating. Such sub regional security organizations were free from any integrationist pretensions and tended to be limited in terms of their goals and memberships."[6]

By early 1990s regionalism was at its peak. The end of the cold war combined with the European Community revitalization programmes carried out through the Single European Act put the 'region' in the centre-stage of international politics. The first factor, in particular, "has lessened the impact of global factors in world politics and has increased the weight of regional forces that had operated all along under the surface of superpowers confrontations."[7] This is manifested in the emergence of a number of new regional organizations such as APEC, LAFTA, etc. and also through the resurgence and reforming of the existing ones.

As mentioned earlier EC/EU is among the better-known regional organizations. It has profound impact on the European affairs in the past five decades through its approaches to integration as applicable to different facets of regional cooperation such as agriculture, commerce, industry, monetary, political, etc. aspects. Its relative success is projected often as a role model for other regional organizations.

Initially created to bind French and German Steel and Coal production under a common authority outside the control of national government, EC/EU, today has come a long way to incorporate economic, political and security aspects of integration. It started with the integration of the economic aspects of society without the inclusion of the high politics. This exemplified the functional approach to regional organization that begins with non-political cooperative arrangement and then could eventually lead to the political integration with passage of time.

Several questions arising in this backdrop are significant. What is the historical backdrop in which EU developed? What are the landmarks in the historical evolution of the EU? How distinct is EU in terms of structures, their powers and decision-making procedures? To what extent and in what manner has the EU responded to the changing needs of its membership as well as those remaining outside it? And what lessons does the example of EU offer to the future evolution of regional organizations, in particular, and international organizations, in general? The study will seek to explore the above questions in six chapters that follow.

The second chapter takes the milestones in the evolutionary process of the EU, the Treaty of Paris, Rome Treaty, the Single European Act and the Maastricht.

The third chapter focuses on the functional, structural and procedural aspects of the EU: major organs, their compositions, functions; decision-making procedures; bureaucracy; and membership enlargement.

The fourth chapter examines the EU's responses to changing needs of members in terms of CAP, monetary policy, and adjustment to the expectation from non-member countries both the developing and developed one alike.

The fifth chapter examines the two new policy areas of the EU, namely, the Common Foreign and Security Policy and the Justice and Home Affairs, introduced in the Maastricht Treaty.

The six and last chapter embodies concluding observations which may open new vista for further research in this field.

The study adopts descriptive and analytical tools. The sources for the study are various EU official publications, published sources, articles in journal and newspaper clippings.

NOTES

1. Inis Claude, *Swords into Ploughshare,* (New York, 1971), p. 105
2. *Ibid.*
3. Davidson Nicol, *Regionalism and New International Economic Order*, (New York, 1981), p. 11
4. John Stoessinger, *The Might of the Nation,* (New York, 1969), p. 302
5. Joseph Nye, *Peace in Parts,* (Boston, 1971), p. 5
6. Louise Fawcett, "Regionalism in historical perspective" in Louise Fawcett and Andrew Hurrell eds, *Regionalism and*

World Politics: Regional Organisation and International order, (Oxford, 1995), p. 16

7. Peter J. Katzenstein, "Regionalism in Comparative perspectives," *Cooperation and Conflicts*, (Stockholm, 1996), vol.31, p.126

2

ORIGIN OF THE EUROPEAN UNION

Its Historical and Political Underpinings

The movement for European Unity is not a new phenomenon, although it would be wrong to characterize current development as a direct descendent of the earlier ideas and proposals. There has been a sporadic attempt since the 8th century AD to unite Europe by forceful means - Charlemagne in the 8th century A.D, in the 19th century A.D Napoleon sought to unite the Continent under the French hegemony and in the 20th century, Hitler tried to subjugate Europe under the dictatorship of the Third Reich.

Apart from the forceful method applied to unite Europe, scholars have also advocated peaceful means of unifying Europe since the Middle Ages. Prominent scholars such as Bentham, Rousseau and Saint-Simon had argued for an institutional form of federal unity in Europe. But despite the existence of such model for European unification, there was resurgence of nationalism in the late 19th century and early 20th century, which eventually culminated into the two World Wars.

During the inter war period, as the decline of the old continent (Europe) became more and more prominent, attempts were made to unify Europe through peaceful means, most notably within the forum of Pan European Movement.

In 1923, Count Coudenhove Kalergi, the Austrian leader and the main pioneer of European integration between wars, called for the creation of the 'United State of Europe'[1] based on example of the United State of America (1776), unification of Switzerland (1648) and the unification of German Empire in 1871. On 29 September 1929, in a famous speech before the League of Nations Assembly in Geneva, the French Foreign Minister Aristide Briand, with the support of his German counterpart, Gustav Stresseman, proposed the creation of 'European Union' within the framework of the League of Nations in order to promote closer cooperation between states of Europe, but without involving any ceding of national sovereignty. However, even before any of the proposals could materialize, Europe was again engulfed by another war thus abruptly halting any further progress.

After the World War II the move towards European Unification stemmed from three main factors. Firstly, there was a shift in the balance of power away from Europe towards the newly emerging superpower, i.e. USA and USSR. Secondly, the earnests desire for peace in the world. Lastly, to avoid the repetition of the earlier mistakes that of military conflicts.

In the pre-war regime, Europe had enslaved and colonised a large part of the inhabited world, which had contributed enormously to their economic prosperity. The transfer of wealth from these colonies to the mother countries had enabled Europe to enjoy prosperity and a measure of democracy. However, the World War II had brought an end to this old order, which was aggravated by the emergence of economic giants like the USA and the Soviet Union, thus pushing Europe to the periphery of the world industrial and economic map. This was manifested by the drop in Europe's share of world industrial goods from roughly half to little more than a quarter by 1950.[2] Not only has its share in world productivity decline, Europe come to depend on USA for the reconstruction of its war-ravaged economy which took the form of "Marshall Plan".[3] The Organisation for European Economic Cooperation (OEEC) which, later on came to be known as the Organisation of Economic Cooperation and Development (OECD), was set up in 1948 for the effective utilisation of the economic aid provided by the US through the Marshall Plan.

As noted, the aftermath of the war witnessed the emergence of the USA and the Soviet Union not only as a superior economic power but also militarily, professing hostile ideologies. The expansionist nature of the Soviet ideology threatened the democratic countries of the Western Europe, who turned to US for protection. The result was the intensification of the cold war, which threatened to bring Europe to the throes of another war. Thus, for Europe, wary of both the Communist expansion and dependence on US and consequent loss of their political autonomy, integration through supranational institution become the clearly perceived need, "to bring an end the demoralising situation in which Europe was at the mercy of political decision taken by other outside Europe."[4]

As such the idea of a politically united Europe was gaining ground towards the late 1940s and 1950s although amid contradictory views. Some felt that France in concert with Belgium and Holland could form the nucleus of European Economic Union, while others thought that United Europe without Russia would be incomplete. Still there were some groups who considered Russia to be a threat on political democracy.[5] However, when confronted with the serious practical proposals towards the idea of politically united Europe, some flinched away from the necessary surrender of national sovereignty and not until the establishment of European Coal and Steel Community (ECSC) in 1952, was there any organisation with supra-national characteristic.

The formation of ECSC was preceded by formation of a number of inter-governmental organisations, which have bearing on the subsequent development in one way or the other. These organisations can be put into three broad categories. The first type was those which have North American involvement such as the Organisation of Economic Co-operation and Development (1948), the North Atlantic Treaty Organisation (1949), the Brussel Pact (1948) and the Western European Union. The second type of organisation aimed to attract as many members as possible and represented by the Council of Europe. The last type of organisation was economic in nature such as OEEC and the ECSC itself. Among these, the Council of Europe was the most politically-oriented organisation with great potential. However, due to prevailing of conflicting views within the organisation, it was never endowed with real power so as to represent an advance towards common institutions.

Despite the existence, and to some extend due to the existence of inter-governmental organisation, the effort at European integration with supra-national institutions did not lose momentum, especially, at the individual and group level. In September 1946, the British Prime Minister, Winston Churchill called for the creation of the United State of Europe, şinging out French and German cooperation as an essential requisite, with Britain as a mere promoter rather than active participant. The impetus for European Union on group level was provided by formation of the European Union of Federalists, which held its first Congress at Montreaux in August 1947. Although it stood for a truly 'United State' two different approaches prevailed within the organisation. The first group led by Altiero Spenelli was the more idealists of the two and called for taking immediate steps towards full political union, established by means of a European Constituent Assembly. For them the time was ripped for political integration of Europe—a final realisation of an age-old mission.[6] On the other hand, the advocates of the second approach were more conservatives and gradualists. They considered Constituent Assembly in 1947 rather premature and advocated an approach based on integration by sectors and on first seeking the support of the key political groups in the countries of Western Europe as an important step in the desired direction.[7] This approach forms the basis for European integration.

2.1 Creation of European Coal and Steel Community (ECSC)

A new chapter in the evolution of integration in Europe was opened in May 1950, when Robert Schuman issued a declaration called the 'Schuman Plan' drawn by Jean Monnet on behalf of the former. The plan, which was to become the precursor of the ECSC, was shaped around the proposal to place French and German coal and steel production under a common authority outside the national control and open to participation from any European states that so wished. The immediate aim was the supranational control of the two commodities whereas the underlying aim was that of future federation in Europe. On this aspect, Jean Monnet wrote: "By pooling of basic production and establishment of a new High Authority whose decisions will be binding on France, Germany and the countries that join them, the proposal will lay the first foundation of European Federation which is indispensable to the maintenance of peace."[8]

The critical factor in this development was the Franco-German reconciliation. The aftermath of the war provide France with an opportunity for a dramatic change of policy towards Germany by giving up the policy of reparation and annexation in favour of Europeanisation of the 'German problem'. This was made crystal clear by Andre Philip, a socialist leader in France, when he said 'the only way to ensure that the new Germany shall not dominate Europe is that Europe dominates the Ruhr'.[9]

Germany agreed to the Declaration the same day, which was soon followed by Italy and the three Benelux countries - Belgium, Luxembourg and the Netherlands. After a prolonged negotiation, the Treaty of Paris, establishing the ECSC was signed in April 1951. With this the Declaration became a reality and after the ratification by the national parliament the Treaty entered into forced in July 1952. The major innovative feature of the Community as compared to other organisations was that its members have ceded to it a part of their national sovereignty, with the goal of forming a cohesive, indissoluble organisational and political unit. In other words, the Community was endowed with sovereign power of its own, independent of the member states, which can adopt acts that have the force of national law.

As mentioned earlier, the aim of the Treaty was not just the creation of a free trade area but also the laying down of the foundation of a common market for coal and scrap[10] This involves the abolition of internal custom duties and quantitative restriction on the imports and exports, measures and practices which discriminate between producers, purchasers, government aids and subsidiaries and restrictive practices tending towards the sharing or exploiting markets. For the smooth realisation of its objectives, the Treaty created four main institutions with a certain degree of supranationalism: 1. High Authority, 2.Council of Ministers, 3. Common Assembly and 4. Cout of Justice. These four institutions with other will be discussed in detail in the next chapter.

From the beginning, the ECSC has been conceived as a success. However, this initial euphoria was short lived as the six failed to ratify the Treaty establishing the European Defense Community and the Draft Statute for European Political Community. The triggering factor was German rearmament, which became necessary because of the outbreak of the Korean War and the intensification of East-

West conflict. However, past experience shows that rearmed Germany could not be tolerable for its neighbour, particularly France. Thus, in October 1950, Rene Pleven, the then French Prime Minister launched a proposal calling for the creation of a European Army under the authority of the political institution of a United Europe.[11] Known as the Pleven Plan, the objective was to bind Germany into a supra-national Community covering defence which would ensure adequate control of rearmed German. However, the plan could not materialize, as the French National Assembly refused to ratify, unwilling to countenance such a far-reaching curb on French sovereignty as to relinquish control over the national army.

2.2 Establishment of the European Economic Community (EEC)

The collapse of EDC dealt a severe blow to the efforts aimed at the political unification of Europe. It highlighted the fact that politically sensitive issues were more prone to be resisted. Thus, concentrating on the less charge/contentious issue in the economic realm, the foreign minister of the ECSC countries under the leadership of the Benelux countries launched a new initiative for the 'creation of the United Europe'. Meeting at Messina in Italy, the six concluded that 'the work of establishing a United Europe must be accomplished by developing common institutions, by gradual amalgamation of the various national economies, the creation of common market and progressive coordination of their social policies.[12] The key to this new initiative was that economic integration should precede political integration. Accordingly, a committee was formed to work out the details of the proposal under the chairmanship of Belgian foreign minister, Paul-Henri Spaak. Known as the Spaak Committee, the report formed the basis of the inter-governmental negotiation leading to the two new Communities, the European Economic Community (EEC) and the European Atomic Community

(Eurotom). Signed on 25th March 1957, the treaties came into force on 1st January 1958 after the national parliaments ratified them. Of the two the EEC was more important. The main aims of EEC are:

- to set up a custom union by removing obstacles to the free movement not only of goods but also of peoples, firms, services and capitals and to harmonise conditions under which imports from thirds countries enter the common market by establishing common custom tariff.
- to harmonise national economic policies and apply common policies throughout the whole market, in particular concerning agriculture, industrial competitions, transport and trade with the rest of the world.
- to improve the living conditions of the community citizens and
- to lay down the foundation for political union and economic union.

By signing the EEC and the Eurotom treaties, the six had confirmed their resolution to continue with the integration through supranational activity even if that meant a major rapture in the Western Europe. The turning point was the realisation that, it was in their interest to progress further along the path on which they had embarked with the founding of the ECSC but with a less politically charged question of economic integration.

However, the six had very different motivation and goals in seeking the creation of the Community. For Germany, involvement in the integration process signified its political rehabilitation within the Community along with recovering of sovereignty over the Saarland till then was under the French control. It also provides security against possible threat from the Soviet troops, which were stationed in East

Germany. Economically also, German has more to gain than to lose as EEC would make its European market more secure, substantially reducing the dangers of its reliance on foreign trade. Last, but not the least, German had hoped that European Unification would facilitate German reunification.[13]

For France, founding of economic community that would include German was the political expression of its readiness for reconciliation and its lasting peace. The French feared the resurgence of independent German industrial and hence perhaps military power. At the same time, any discriminatory control against Germany could lead to the recurrence. Therefore, by binding the German with other European countries, France hoped to contain German power skillfully and without imposing an inferior status.[14] Economically, it offered an access to raw materials needed for industrial expansion and opened up new markets.

The economic consideration constituted the main reason for Italy's joining the EEC. Though fairly industrialised, emigration of too many workers usually locked in unproductive employment in agriculture reduced the potential for development of South. Italy had counted on financial assistance from community regional scheme to develop the more backward parts of the country so as to reduce the high level of unemployment. There were political considerations also. Recovering from over twenty years of fascist rule followed with a military defeat, integration offered an opportunity for a new start with dignity.[15]

For the Benelux countries also, the motivation was the post-war reconstruction. It was the economic benefits of securing export markets and establishing and developing new industries that was the main attraction for these countries. Apart from the economic benefit, the desire to be in good terms with West Germany and France, the two big neighbours of the three countries was also another factor.

However, even before the treaties had taken effect, the British government provoked a fierce quarrel within Europe over the best approach to European Economic integration. Apart from its antipathy to supra-nationalism, the British had been unwilling to either a common tariff or the common agriculture policy as it would damage its economic link with the Commonwealth. So, the British idea was to set up a European free trade area between the six and other OECD countries without a common external tariff or arrangement for the harmonisation of laws to prevent distortion of competition. Although Britain was able to win Denmark, Norway, Ireland, Austria, Portugal and Switzerland, the initiative eventually failed in the face of the opposition from the six who were reluctant to jeopardise its achievements by participating simultaneously in a loosely arrangement. Consequently, they formed the European free trade area and later on came to be known as European Economic Area in 1992, after entering into an understanding with the EC, in which the relationship between the two assimilated into internal European Community relationship, and the basic principles of the internal market applicable.

The years following the signing of the EEC treaty was marked by economic boom with unprecedented growth. As a result, despite the lack of monetary power, the community forged ahead with the establishment of the Custom Union. The EEC treaty had provided for 12 years transitional period divided into three stages 4 years each and 1st January 1970 as the date for the realization of the common market. The first two stages went on smoothly and was marked by the removal of protection within the Community, the creation of common external tariff, the liberalization of the free movement of workers, and the creation of a system protecting the social security interests of migrant workers, the adoption of the initial regulation for implementation of Community policy and the introduction of a system of common prices and Common Agriculture Policy (CAP).[16]

However, by the end of the second stage just before the beginning of the third stage, problem arose over some constitutional provisions such as providing Community's own financial resources, expansion or increasing the European Parliament's power and particularly over the decision making process in the Council of Ministers on the replacement of unanimous decision-making by weighted majority voting as provided by the Treaty. Though the problem was resolved following the Luxembourg Compromise, it represented major setback in the process towards European integration and a major victory for inter-governmentalism. Despite the existence of such a major disagreement over an important constitutional issue, there was a common concord among the six to continue working for European integration.

2.3 Toward the Single European Acts (SEA)

The issue of reforming the EC has been permanent topic since the late 1960s. The need for reformation was made more acute by the Luxembourg Compromise, which nearly completely destroyed the effectiveness of the Community decision-making process. Coupling with these was oil crisis of the early 1970s, which put the Community under tremendous stress, as it is not geared efficiently to solve the problem on multilateral scale. The result was the attempt to solve the problem at individual state level through increasing protectionist measures, stalemate of legislative procedure, the failure to implement the proposed monetary union, etc. As such the Community deviated from its ideal: "that it exists to find common solution to common problems."[17]

Thus starting from 1969, efforts had been made to find remedy for such inefficiency. The Hague Conference of the Heads of the States and the Government of December 1969 re-launched the Community by accepting the proposals of giving own financial resources (agriculture included), extension of the Community's competence in monetary integration and widening the Parliamentary powers. It also agreed to revive the Fouchet Plan, which later became the basis for European Political Cooperation (EPC), the Community collective foreign policy was given Treaty base in the SEA.

In 1975, there had been an abortive effort to create European Union, which took the form of Tindemann reports, named after the Belgian Prime Minister Leo Tindemann. The report made a far-reaching recommendation advocating economic and monetary integration, rights of European citizenship, regional and social policies, institutional reforms, and role of European Council and development of the Community's global relation and foreign policy[18]. Though it did not materialised at that time, it formed the basis for both SEA and Maastricht Treaty.

The early 1980s saw the rekindling of the debate, which had been on and off since 1969 Hague Summit. The debate concentrated on three main specific points; future enlargement; budget problems and institutional reforms. The discussion was necessitated by two factors.[19]

First factor was the ineffectiveness of the institution and the paralyses in the decision making process of EC following Luxembourg Compromise, coupled with the fear that further enlargement would lead to a total collapse in the decision making process in council of ministers. And secondly, there was a need for expansion of the European Parliament Powers.

Consequently, the debate concentrated on remedying the existing shortcomings of decision making process, particularly, the lack of transparency and efficiency, and on improving the democratic legitimacy of European policy to political tasks.[20]

All these development since 1969 culminated into negotiation for major revision of the Community treaties, which began at 1984 Fountainbleau Summit and formed the basis for the Single European Act (SEA). The act was preceded by a history characterised by three documents – the Solemn Declaration at Stuttgart Summit, the European Parliament's 1984 Draft Treaty on European Union and Dooge Committee report, all of which invariably revolved around the decision making process in the EC Council and expansion of the powers of Parliament. Of these, the Parliament Draft Treaty was the most ambitious with a design to take qualitative step forward in the process of European integration; to update and expand upon the existing institutional framework for the union; and to render the institutions more democratic, effective and accountable than earlier.[21]

The Fountainbleau Summit was followed by June 1985 Milan Summit in which the major agenda of discussion was the report by Dooge Committee and the Commission's ambitious programme to complete Single Market by the end of 1992. An inter-governmental conference was convened after the Milan Summit to give a treaty base to foreign policy cooperation and revised some institutional arrangement. Amidst opposition from some members, an agreed text emerged by January 1986 and entered into force on 1st July 1987 after the ratification by the member states. The main features of the SEA were implementation of Single Market by the end of 1992, establishment of legal and a number of institutional reforms.[22] It also defined a Community competence in the field of environment, research and technology, internal market and condition at work place; set monetary union as a community objective and importantly it recognised the need for financial support for the weaker economies in the community to enable them to participate in the process of Single Market.[23]

Though undoubtedly, a major achievement, it however was not a treaty that advances European integration *per se*.

It felt short of the supra-nationalist expectation that had hoped for independent decision-making power of European Parliament. But all the same, the SEA did lend a new dimension to the European integration and paved way for 1992 Maastricht Treaty, which finally transformed EC into EU.

2.4 The Maastricht Treaty

The Treaty of Maastricht represents a major breakthrough in the process of European integration. For the first time, the Community had ventured in an issue area: Political integration. This took the form of Common Foreign and Security Policy and Justice and Home Affairs, the second and third pillar of the European Union.

The catalytic factor was the adoption of the 1992 Single Market programme, and the amendment of the treaty of Rome through the SEA, which help in recovering the prestige and effectiveness of the Community. This was reflected in the huge increase in the rate of adoption for legislation and the vigorous pressing ahead of the work of the Single Market programme. Thus beginning from the late 1980s there was a new sense of direction and purpose in European integration. The prospects for European Union come clearly in view stimulated by two factors – internal and external.[24] Internal factors stemmed mainly from the need to move towards European Monetary Union (EMU) in the form of single currency, other factors like the Single European Market (SEM) and SEA had contained integrationist logic in itself by focussing on some long standing but resolved issue facing the community. Also there was a need for a Community 'social dimension' which would soften and offset some of the liberal market or deregulatory implication of SEM; the dismantling of border control in internal market created a new and much improved mechanism at community level to deal with such problems as cross-border crime, drug trafficking, international terrorism, etc., and the need for further institutional reforms.

The external factors arose largely from the break-up of both Soviet bloc and Soviet Union. There were four aspects to this. First, the collapse of Communism in Central and Eastern European Countries in 1989 and the emergence of liberal democracy based on market economy in its place meant that the Community would be dealing with Europe's wide issues and problems. Secondly, the unification of Germany in 1990 and the subsequent inclusion of the East Germany in the Community increased the possibility of New German dominating the Community. It was felt necessary to advance the integration process in order to prevent such happening and to ensure that the future would see European Germany than German Europe. Third, the instability caused by the break-up of the Soviet Union necessitated the strengthening of Community policy and institutional capabilities. Last, but not the least, was that the end of cold war heralded the disappearance of the framework on which the Community owed its existence – that of a compact bloc on defense mechanism against Soviet expansionism. As a result, there was a need for reorientation of the community, reinforced by the inadequate Community response to 1990-91 Gulf War.

From the mid-1988 several factors combined to build up a head of steam for another round of Community deepening. In June 1988 a Committee, chaired by French Statesman Jacques Delors, was formed with a view to identify the concrete stages needed to realise the EMU. Reporting in April 1989, the Committee identified three basic attributes to Monetary Union: full currency convertibility, complete integration of financial market and irrevocable looking of exchange rate.[25] At the same time some member states were demanding significant moves towards political union involving the extension of the competence of the Community and enhancement of the democratic accountability of its institutions.[26] So, in December 1990, the Community leaders formally convened two inter-governmental conferences, the first one to map out the steps needed to establish EMU and the second to deal with the obstacles standing in the way of political union. The outcome of the two intergovernmental conferences was the treaty of Maastricht. The Treaty of European Union was signed in February 1992 and entered into force on 1st November 1993. The ratification process was very protracted, particularly in Denmark, which ratifies the treaty after the second referendum in May 1993. France ratified in 1992 September with a very marginal/ narrow vote in favour (51.05% to 48.95%) while UK delayed ratification till the second referendum in Denmark, and that of Germany's involved legal challenged over the constitutional issues.

The main features of the Maastricht treaty were the incorporation of the principles of subsidiary and union citizenship; strengthening and extending of the Community's policy competence as seen from setting of time table for establishing EMU by the end of 1990s; institutional changes; extension of parliament decision making powers, upgrading of European Council as an open body, etc. The treaty also added two new areas of policy, a Common Foreign and Security Policy (CFSP) and Justice and Home Affairs (JHA) to the original three communities.

The treaty created a new organisation, the European Union based on three pillars – ECs, CFSP and JHA. While the first one operated through supra-national body, the last two are operated by inter-governmental cooperation through the administrative machinery of the Commission.[27] A sort of federal system was created, as a result of a compromise between those who held different views about the future of the European Union. The Pillar concept of the European Union is illustrated in the Fig. 2.1.[28]

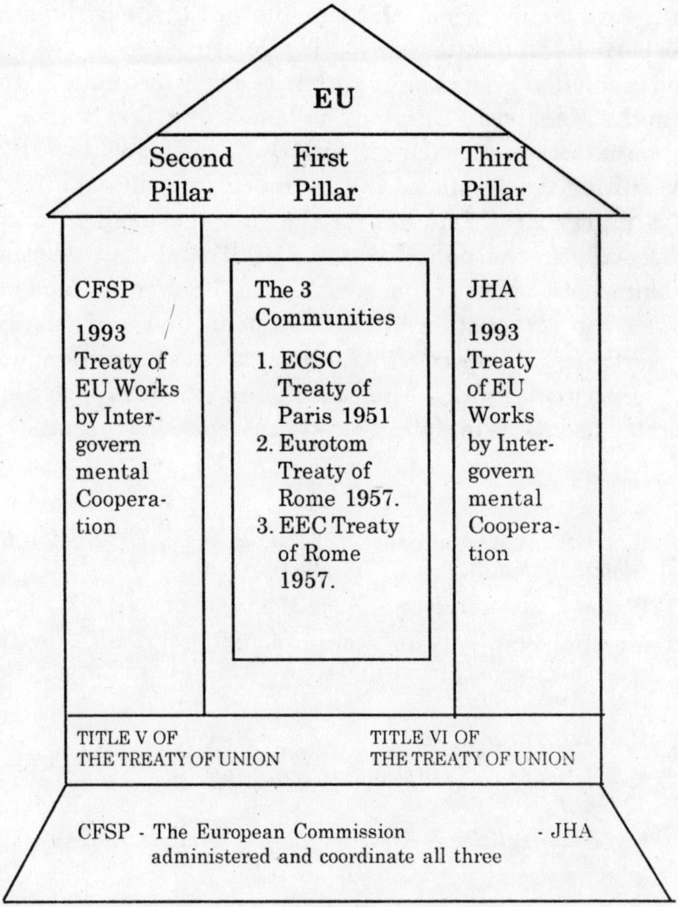

Fig. 2.1

Despite the existence of different views on the process of European integration, the treaty of European Union or the Maastricht Treaty significantly enhances the deepening of the integration process in Western Europe.

The European Union as it exists today has come a long way since its inception as ECSC in 1952. Created as a mean to ensure lasting peace and stability in Europe by binding the participating states irrevocably in custom union, it slowly and gradually bring in more within its fold, which culminated into the Maastricht Treaty. The Maastricht Treaty though represents a watershed in the history of European integration by shifting the emphasis from economic to political affairs, also marked the triumph of the inter-governmentalist. Especially in the policy areas of CFSP and JHA decision making entrusted to inter-governmental conference and not under the jurisdiction of the European Court of Justice. Nevertheless the success in the policy areas such as Common Agricultural policy and European Monetary Union established its formidability in the international arena.

NOTES

1. K.B. Lall, Wolfgang Ernst, H.S. Chopra eds., *The EEC in the Global System,* (New Delhi. 1984), p. 10.
2. Walter Hallstein, *Europe in the Making,* (London, 1972), p.19.
3. Marshal Plan was an American Aid Programme for the economic reconstruction and recovery of Western Europe after the II World War.
4. Hallstcin, n. 2, p. 19.
5. H.S. Chopra, *De Gualle and European Unity,* (New Delhi, 1979), p. 7.
6. G. Smith, *Politics in Western Europe,* (Heinemann, 1972), p. 305.
7. David Combes, *Politics and Bureaucracy in European Community,* (London, 1970), p. 18.
8. Martin Holland, *European Integration,* (London, 1993), p. 25.
9. F.R.Willis, *France, Germany and the New Europe*: 1945–67. (Oxford, 1968), p. 58.
10. Treaty Establishing the ECSC, Article- 4.
11. Neill Nugent, *The Politics and the Government of the European Union,* (London, 1995), p. 43.
12. Stanley Henig, *The Uniting of Europe: From Discord to Concord* (London, 1997), p. 27.

13. Chopra, *op.cit.* pp. 137-138.
14. John Pinder, "European Community and Nation States: Case of Neo-federalism", *International Affairs,* (London), Vol.62, no.1, Winter, 1985, p. 42.
15. Chopra, *op.cit.,* pp. 137-138.
16. Jo Shaw, *Law of European Union,* 2nd edition, (London, 1996), p. 34.
17. Edward Heath, "European unity over the next 10 years: From Community to Union", *International Affairs,* (London), vol.64, no.1, Spring 1988, p. 200.
18. Holland, *op.cit.,* p. 41
19. Werner Weidenfeld, " Single European Act", *Aussen Politik,* Vol.-37, no.4 (Hamburg, 1986) p. 389.
20. *Ibid.*
21. Juliet Lodge, *The European Community in Search of Future,* (London, 1986), p. 8.
22. Henig, *op.cit.,* p. 76.
23. Pinder, *op.cit.,* p. 45.
24. Nugent, *op.cit.,* pp. 57-59.
25. Shaw, *op.cit.,* p. 47.
26. *Ibid,* p. 48.
27. S.F. Goodman, *The European Union,* (London, 1996) p. 7.
28. *Ibid.,* p. 8.

3

STRUCTURAL AND FUNCTIONAL ASPECTS OF THE EUROPEAN UNION

This chapter deals with the structural, functional and procedural aspects of the EU, such as membership, enlargement, organs, decision-making procedure, etc.

The structure or organs of an organisation are the physical manifestation of the intentions of the members of the organisation. They are formalised structure, normally provided for by the constitution through which an overall power of an organisation is exercised. It is through these organs that an organisation tries to achieve its aims and aspirations and at the same time ligitimises its activities. So, when ECSC was established in 1952, the treaty had provided for four main organs: the High Authority, the Council of Ministers, the Common Assembly and the Court of Justice. These four organs along with a new institution—the Court of Auditors, were latter incorporated when the EEC was established. Apart from these five major organs, there are many subsidiary bodies; some came along as the Union has developed. The uniqueness of these organs is that each member act as the representative of the member states whether they are elected, appointed or sent by the member nations and has supranational power. However, before going deeper into the discussion on these organs, it will be better to discuss the aspects of EU membership.

3.1 Aspects of EU Membership

The enlargement of the EU membership is an ongoing process. From the first membership application of Britain, Denmark, Ireland and Norway in 1961 to the application of the Central and Eastern European Countries (CEEC) who joined the EU in 2004, the Union has been constantly considering, negotiating or absorbing the impact of accessions of one or more members and thereby increasing the cultural, social and economic heterogeneity of the Union. This openness of the EU to additional membership was evident from the very day the 'Schuman Plan' was declared with an open invitation to any state that wished to participate. This was re-emphasised in the Maastricht Treaty, however, with a 'pre-condition tag' that of democracy and market economy.

The first application for full membership came from Britain, Denmark, Ireland and Norway in 1961 itself. Shedding off its initial skepticism on Economic Community, Britain applied for membership in 1961 and was followed by the other three countries. There were two factors responsible behind the consideration of its stand by Britain. First was the initial success of EEC as compare to its own economic performance and the second was the dwindling of British influence in the world political arena as most of her former colonies became independent and championed their own cause and hence were less inclined to acknowledge British leadership. With the independent of former colonies, British economic position deteriorated and a massive balance of payment destroyed any prospects for economic growth while the Community began to show growth rate of five per cent.[1] At the same time EFTA was an unsuitable platform to revive its imminent position because of its purely economic objective and it was felt that Britain risked political isolation by remaining outside the Community. This was reinforced by need to protect its existing market and to open new ones as a result of changing pattern of world trade. Hence, the rapid growing Community market offered an ideal opportunity for mobilizing and revitalizing its economy.

For the Scandinavian countries, the attraction for membership stemmed from the economic gain they could get through the free trade. Denmark, a major producer of food was on the look out for market where it could export the surpluses at guaranteed prices. This along with the British application, the largest import market of Denmark, formed the strongest factor behind its application. The Irish saw entry into the Community as a chance to boast its vital farm export. Its English export market was not large enough to exploit its full potential. In addition, there was a need for new markets for it's newly growth industries. The Community social and regional fund was another point of attraction

The negotiations that followed ran until January 1963 but broke off abruptly when De Gualle exercise French veto because of his deep mistrust of the intention behind the British application, the first of its kind that put a break in the integration process of Europe. Undaunted of such political rebuff from the France, they applied once again in 1967. Once again, the attempt floundered against French reservation. It was only in 1969, after the fall of De Gualle, that a breakthrough came about in Hague Summit which opened the application for consideration. After a lengthy negotiation, the treaties of accession was signed on 22nd January 1972 and on 1st January 1973, after successful referenda in Ireland and Denmark and ratification by National Parliament—Britain, Ireland and Denmark became the full members of the Community. Norway, however, rejected the membership in its referendum by 53.49 per cent votes.[2] The member of the Community/Union was thus increased from six to nine.

The second wave of membership application came from the Southern and less developed regions of the Continent, i.e, Greece in 1975 and Spain and Portugal in 1977.

Prior to the military regime, Greece was an associate member of the Community/Union. After the restoration of democracy, Greece opted for full membership instead of going for associate status again. As such Greece applied for membership in 1975. It saw full membership as a means to stabilize its newly restored democracy. Economically, it hoped to be a net recipient from EU budget[3] and modernized its agriculture and industries which would lead to economic development. After overcoming the widely held reservation about encroachment upon national sovereignty and the fear of increased foreign intervention in Greek domestic affairs, a treaty of accession was signed on 28th May 1977 which came into force on 1st January 1981, thus making Greece the tenth member of the Community/Union.

Negotiations were more protracted with Spain and Portugal as some members, particularly France, expressed reservation because of vast economic gap. But, the fact that both the countries have returned to democracy after an arbitrary neo-fascist, work in favour of these countries. And on 12th June 1985 after signing the treaties of accession and ratification by twelve parliaments, the two countries became the member of the Community, enlarging its members to twelve.

Apart from the obvious economic benefits the Community membership entailed, there were political attractions for the membership. For Spain, it was the fulfilment of a long standing ambition of ending its political isolation within Europe while for Portugal;, it meant a return to its original European roots after the lost of its colonies and domestic political upheaval.[4]

The third wave and the last for 20th century of enlargement came in 1995. It was precipitated by the end of cold war and the broke up of the Soviet Bloc. With the collapse of the elsewhere Soviet Union, there has been a number of applicants for EU membership- Austria (July 1989); Sweden (July 1991); Finland (March 1992) and Norway (November 1992). The accession negotiations were formally opened with Austria, Finland and Sweden in 1992 and that of Norway in 1993. By 1994, a treaty was concluded in Brussels which became effective in 1995 after the successful referendum held in each of the countries. However, Norway once again rejected membership by 52.4 per cent.[5]

The motivating factors behind their membership application were both political and economic. During the cold war era these countries had practiced the policy of neutrality and took great care to cultivate balance relation with both East and West. The end of cold war had brought an end to this necessity and thus leaving these countries free to apply for membership without fearing repercussion from Soviet Union. Economic factor stemmed from dissatisfaction of these countries with EU. Though essentially bound together through the creation of industrial free trade areas since 1992, overtime EU was collectively much stronger than EFTA.

There are two more groups of potential members—the Mediterranean applicants—Cyprus, Turkey and Malta and CEECs—Bulgaria, the Czech Republic, Estonia, Hungary, Latvia, Lithuania, Poland, Slovakia, Slovenia and Romania.

The membership applications from the Mediterranean had been received as early as 1987—Turkey (1987), Cyprus and Malta (1990) but has been put aside in 1995 enlargement. In case of Malta and Cyprus, it was partly because of the reluctance on the part of the Union to tackle institutional questions involved in the accession of small states and the desire to resolve the problem of Turkish occupation of Northern Cyprus before accession could be contemplated.[6] As for Turkey, the problem includes over-sized population, ignorance even among the political elites about the European integration beyond the desire for membership and the suspicious that it may turn into a strong defender of its national interest.[7]

Regarding the CEECs, the problems derived mainly from their low level of economic development which could hold back the pace of European integration. The Copenhagen European Council (1993) had laid down certain conditions as eligibility criteria for membership. They are:

1. Stable government which guarantee democracy, the rule of law, human rights and respect and protection for minorities.
2. Existence of market economy capable of withstanding competition from the Union; and
3. The ability to sign upto the objectives of the Union.

Though, the condition of establishing democratic institutions is fulfilled, there are problems regarding the last two conditions. Being under command economy for so long, the CEECs lack basic institutions for modern market economy such as price system that reflect market factors, a stable central bank and commercial banks, a fixed laws of property and contract, a stock exchange lawyer and accountancy firms, profit oriented enterprises, managers and exporters and administrators of firms in bankruptcy without which a Single Market cannot exist.[8]

At the same time motivation for membership application stemmed from the economic rationale of seeking financial help to aid their transition to market economies and the security reasons based around trying to free themselves from any Russian influence[9] rather than shared common objectives of the European federation.

There are also other problems such as relatively low levels of economic development, high population, institutional problems, particularly the Commission and the Parliament plus the unwillingness of the CEECs to accept the acquis communataire.

Despite all these problems, the EU has began to officially embark on discussion with six countries i.e., Poland, Hungary, the Czech Republic, Slovenia, Estonia and Cyprus in March 1998 and another six counties- Slovakia, Latvia, Lithuania, Malta, Romania and Bulgaria followed suit two years latter. After a marathon negotiation, these 10 countries except Romania and Bulgaria finally signed treaty of accession on 16th April 2003 at a ceremony in Athens,[10] the cradle of the European democracy. The 25 leaders of the existing and the future EU members signed the treaty. The treaty come into force on 1st January 2004 after successful ratification by parliaments in all 15 EU countries plus national referenda in all the candidate countries except Cyprus.[11] With the joining of 10 more countries 75 million people is being added to EU and thus ending East-West division of the continent.

The Five Major Organs of the EU

EU is built on an institutional system which is the only one of its kind in the world. The member-states delegate sovereignty for certain matter to independent institutions which represent the interest of the Union as a whole, its member countries and its citizens.

As mentioned earlier, there are five major organs of the EU—the Commission, the Parliament, the Council of Ministers, the Court of Justice and the Court of Auditors. The Commission traditionally upholds the interest of the Union as a whole, while each national government is represented in the Council and the European Parliament is directly elected by the people, which is another unique characteristic of EU institutional set-up. Two more institutions: the Court of Justice and the Court of Auditors flank this institutional triangle of Commission, Council and European Parliament. Besides these five major organs, there are also five other European bodies/ organs which we will discuss one by one in this chapter. In addition 13 specialized agencies have also been set up to handle certain essentially technical, scientific or management tasks.

3.2 The Council of Ministers

The Council of Ministers is the principal and ultimate decision-making body of the EU. It has a dual nature. It is supra-national on the one hand and inter-governmental on the other. It consists of representatives of all the member states authorized to commit the government of the member-states. It is the institution through which the national interests of the member-states is represented and is responsible to the national parliament.

The Council is presided over for a period of six months by each member states in turn in accordance with the pre-established rule (unless a new council decision is taken). During its presidency; the member state has lot of responsibilities as well as power. As President of the Council, the head of that member state has to meet leaders and dignitaries of other states regarding matter related to the EU. It also has the power to decide which matter should be given priority, what agenda should be taken up or when to call meetings. Recently, the question of permanent and elected EU President cropped up, as the bloc grapple with vital reforms and the drafting of its first ever constitution. The members of the EU were widely divided regarding this institutional reform. While bigger countries such as Britain, France and Spain are in favour of this reform, the smaller countries in the EU such as Austria, Belgium, Ireland, Luxembourg, the Netherlands and Portugal were against such reform. In this regard, Luxembourg Prime Minister Jean

Claude Junker told news conference that 'there is no reason to endow with this new institution in which an elected President of EC would rake over from the present system of rotating six-month Presidency.' This opposition may have been stemmed from the anxiety that if bigger countries hold the post permanently, the interest of the smaller EU countries may be overshadowed in the long run. However, this does not mean that all the smaller EU countries are against it. Denmark and Finland are all for the reform while Greece as the then President of the Council cannot voice its opinion.

The work of the Council is divided into different policy areas for instance, General Affair, Agriculture, etc. Each of the 15 (now 27) member-state government is represented by minister responsible for the subject area in question. In practice, this composition is not strictly followed and depends on the availability of the ministers responsible and on the difficulty or the seriousness of the issue under discussion.

The Council of Ministers is assisted by a small national delegation composed of national officials and experts and sometimes by junior ministers ranging from five to nine members. The number varied according to the policy area concerned, the importance of the items on agenda and the size of the room.[12] Their function is to ensure that the head of the delegation is properly briefed about the items to be discussed.[13]

A Committee of Permanent Representatives from member-states assists the Council, colloquially known as the COREPER. It is made up of all national civil servants covering all major policy. It works in conjunction with the official from relevant national ministries and is headed by the Permanent Representative who acts as a kind of ambassador.

There are two types of COREPER: COREPER I and COREPER II.

COREPER I: Preparation of Internal Market; Energy Research; Industry; Telecommunication; Fisheries; Transport; Environment; Labour and Social Affairs; Health, Education and Culture; Tourism and Agriculture. It is composed of Deputy Permanent Representative.

COREPER II: Preparation of Institutional matters; General Affairs; Development, Justice and Home Affairs and Budget Council meetings. It is composed of Permanent Representatives.

The main purpose of COREPER is to negotiate and reach agreement on proposals and policies and thus lessen the burden of discussion at ministerial level.

In performing their duty the Council and the COREPER are assisted by a complicated network of committees and working group consists of national official, sectional interest groups or experts from national government.

Council decision-making Process

There are three basic ways in which the Council takes decisions: qualified majority, simple majority and unanimously. The same pattern is used in Parliament also.

As a rule the Council is obliged to take decision on the basis of proposals from the Commission which are intimated through the Council's Secretariat. As soon as the General Secretariat receives the Commission's proposal, the relevant working party meeting is convened on the instruction of the COREPER.[14] It examines and produces common stand on the proposal with no decision being taken. After this, the working party's document is referred to the COREPER. Even at this level no decision is taken except for decision to initiate written procedural decision.

The third stage is the ministerial meeting where the formal adoption of the Council legislation takes place. The items in this meeting are divided into two categories. The first category items consist of those issues which have been agreed in the COREPER and do not required any further discussion. The second category items are those issues that could not be resolved in COREPER meeting because of its sensitivity and political nature.

During the Council meetings discussion take the form of either discussion leading to a decision or policy debates or points of information for the Council.

After the discussion, decisions are taken either unanimously or by voting. Unanimous decision taking is applied in dealing with revenue, taxation and social policy while in other areas such as transport, environment and other matters related to the establishment of the internal market voting is applied.[15]

3.3 The Commission

The Commission is the main driving force behind the European integration. It initiates and implements policies, acts as a watchdog of the treaties and participates in decision-making.

There are 20 members in the European Commission drawn from fifteen EU member states, two each from five larger states, i.e., Germany, France, Britain, Italy and Spain and one each from the other ten. But after the accession of 10 more members the number has increase to 27, one each from 27 members. They are chosen on ground of their general competence and independence beyond doubt. They all constitute the College of the Commissioners.

The Commissioners are appointed by the member states for a renewable five years term with the approval of the parliament. Although chosen by a member government, each one of them swears an oath of independence to keep off from home country's influence.

The Commissioners once appointed has a security of tenure. No one, not even Parliament has the power to dismiss an individual Commissioner on ground of being difficult or inefficient. However, if a member of Commission is found lack in integrity, the Court of Justice on the application by the Council or the Commission can dismiss him or her.[16] In addition to this, the Parliament also has the right to censure the Commission as a whole which it tried to in one occasion (1999) but had failed.

The Commissioners are assisted by cabinets (which operates outside the formal bureaucracy of the Commission) composed of officials personally appointed by the Commissioner mostly from his or her native country. Headed by the *Chef de Cabinet,* the size of the Cabinet ranges from six to twelve. The main task of the Cabinet is to assist the Commissioner with his policy responsibilities, enabling the public image and political philosophy, administrative coordination and liaising with member states.[17] The Cabinet of the President has extra responsibility of 'brokering the different views and interest which exist amongst Commissioners and in Commission as a whole, so as to ensure that as an institution the Commission is clear, coherent and efficient.[18]

Powers and Function of the Commission

The powers and functions of the Commission are laid down in Article 155(c) of the EC Treaty. They are discussed under four heads:

1. Initiating proposals for legislation;
2. Executive and administrative power;
3. Representation of EU interest; and
4. Guardian of the Treaty.

The Commission has the right to initiate proposal for legislation in the decision-making procedure without which there cannot be any legislation. Only Commission can initiate such proposal with occasional direction from the Council or the Parliament. This right is an exclusive one in the areas cover by the first pillar of EU but is a diluted one where second and third pillars are concerned.

There are three ways in which Commission develops the policy of EU—through proposals for action, drafting of budget and taking policy decision.[19]

The Commission has a wide range of administrative and executive function such as rule making, implementation of EU policies and management of finance.

Rule making is a power delegated by the Council to the Commission to lay down rules to be followed by national administration. In its exercise of this power, a committee called 'Comitology' made up by representatives of the member states supervises the Commission. Comitology is the outcome of member states desire to preserve the national influence beyond the legislative role of the Council itself and the Community's desire to speed up decision by more frequent delegation to the Commission the power to implement Community legislation.[20]

In implementing the EU policies, the Commission is faced with many problems. One such problem is the shortage of staff. As a result there is few cases of direct implementation by the Commission and has to rely heavily on the goodwill of the national government for carrying out its task.

As a manager of EU finances, the Commission keeps a watch on both revenue collection and expenditure, coordinates, manages the finances which are not drawn exclusively from EU sources such as environment programme etc.

Another important function of the Commission is to ensure that the member-states and the interested groups within the EU comply with the treaties and legislation made under EU. This it does through both supervision and direct enforcement. As a supervisor the Commission's task is to detect breaches of Community law while as an enforcer its job is to take action by bringing the proceeding to the European Court of Justice. However, before bringing to the Court of Justice, it tries to resolve the problem by persuading, cajoling and negotiating with the errant party. The Commission has the power to take decision on its own in a number of areas. In the field of Competition Policy, it has the power to raid the offices of any company suspected of breaching the law.[21]

The Commission is also responsible for representing the EU in the international arena. In this capacity the President who is responsible for attending international conferences, maintaining bilateral link with the non- member country, represents it by sending and receiving delegates etc. At the same time, it has to uphold 'European View' at the time of clash of interest between national government and the Union.

3.4 European Parliament (EP)

European Parliament is the only directly elected institution of the EU, the largest multinational Parliament in the world.

It comprises of 626 members from 15, (now 785 from 27) EU member states. These seats are allocated according to the size and population of the states and at the same time ensuring that the voice of the smallest state is heard. Allocations of seats are as follows:

EU-15

Germany	99
Italy	87

France	87
UK	87
Spain	64
The Netherlands	31
Belgium	25
Greece	25
Portugal	25
Sweden	22
Austria	21
Denmark	16
Finland	16
Ireland	15
Luxembourg	6

The Members of Parliament (MEP) are elected by direct universal suffrage since 1979. Before it, they were ministers delegated from each member state's Parliament. Except for Britain, the MEPs are elected on the basis of one or the other form of proportional representation. The Parliament mainly comprises of varied political groups such as Socialist group, Christian Democrats, Group of Green, etc., which are relatively very influential. For instance, in the early 1999 when the Parliament had called for ensuring motion against the Commission, the motion was defeated by 293 votes to 232 mostly cast by the Socialist group and the Christian Democrats, the largest group respectively in the Parliament at that time.[22]

Nineteen committees and four sub-committees carry out most of the Parliament workload. All the MEPs are full member of at least one committee and sometimes of the sub-committees. The main task of the committee is to examine legislature proposal which require EP opinion. The committees are also required to explore ideas with the Commission, foster own initiatives and discuss developments with the President in office.[23]

The Parliament has four decision-making bodies: Plenary, Bureau, Enlarge Bureau and College of Quaestors. The Parliament has no single site and is dispersed in three different cities—Strasbourg, Brussels and Luxembourg. As such the meetings of these four decision-making bodies are held in different places.

Plenary sessions are held in Strasbourg throughout the year except in August. In addition to these sessions four to five mini Plenaries are held in Brussels. The agenda for the Plenaries is drafted by the appropriate committee and then recommended by the President and Enlarge Bureau in consultation with Conference of Committee Chairman and the Secretariat. For each proposal a rapporteur is appointed from the appropriate committee with the responsibility to produce a draft resolution. Only those issues that are urgent and sensitive are discussed in the Plenary over one or two time slots with maximum three hours discussion in total.

Voting is a personal right and no proxy voting is allowed. Voting is done both by show of hand and through electronic machines. Parliament adopts legislation by following any of the three types of voting-simple majority, qualified majority and unanimity,[24] same as that of the Council decision-making.

The Parliamentary Bureau comprises of a President, fifteen Vice-Presidents and five Quaestors acting in an advisory capacity. They are elected from amongst the MEP for the period of two and half years. Each group has different roles of which the role of the President is the most important. It ranges from presiding and closing Parliament sitting, chairing the meetings of the Bureau and Enlarged Bureau, representing the Parliament in and outside the Union, managing the day to day running and administrative structure and signing the Union's budget.

The functions of the Vice-President are to take over the President's place in his absence and to take part in the meeting of the Bureau and Enlarged Bureau. The Quaestors manage administration and finances which directly concern the MEP, take part in Bureau and Enlarged Bureau meetings as an advisor and look after a specific policy area.

Since 1993, the Enlarged Bureau was replaced by Conference of President of the Parliament (no vote) and the Chairman of the political groups or their representatives. The main task of the new body is to find consensus on matter referred to it and in case of failure to reach consensus voting is done with a weightage based on the number of members in each political groups.[25]

Both the Bureau and Enlarged Bureau have two meeting a month, one during each Plenary session and the other between Plenaries. Both have the power to take decision. Bureau decisions mainly concern financial matters and Parliament staff issues while that of the Enlarged Bureau includes relations with the non EU institutions and organizations and relation with other institutions and bodies of the Union. As far as possible decisions are taken by consensus but voting is also done when necessary. The meeting of the Quaestors is, by far, the most frequent one and took place before the two and has no final decision making power.

Functions and Powers of the Parliament

The EP has undergone gradual changes since its inception. Initially, it had only consultative powers, but now with the help of certain procedures which were introduced in the subsequent treaties; it participates in the actual decision making process of the EU.

The power of the Parliament can be divided into three categories: legislative power, budgetary power and supervisory power over executive.

The legislative power of the Parliament has been expanding since the inception of the EU. The first such expansion was conferring of budgetary power in 1970 and 1975 amending treaties over the concerned for democratic control of the Union expenditure.[26] The subsequent treaties of the Union strengthened and extended the legislative power of the Parliament which can be used with the aid of various procedures such as cooperation procedure, assent procedure, co-decision procedure, consultative procedure and special procedure.[27]

As noted earlier, the Parliament acquired its first budgetary power in 1970. Since then the power has been consolidated through the treaties or by agreements between the institutions. These powers range from approving the Union's budget, proposition of modification and amendment to Commission's initial proposals and to the position taken by member states in the Council to expenses on education, social programmes, etc.[28] It also has the exclusive power to sign the Union budget into law. It, however, does not have any say on the compulsory expenditure of the Union eg. expenses of the institutions etc.

Both the Commission and the Council share the executive function of the Union and are responsible to the Parliament though in a limited way. As such the Parliament exercises a wide range of control and supervision over the Commission and to some extend over the Council.

Parliament control over Commission is already discussed under the Commission heading. However here it is worth mentioning a recent and unprecedented happening, of the resignation of the Commission as a whole in March 1999. After the failure of the censure motion against the

Commission initiated by the Parliament in January 1999, the Parliament appointed a Committee of Experts including judges to investigate the existence of alleged mal-administration within the Commission. The finding of the Committee confirmed the allegation, though it did not directly accused the Commissioners except Edith Cresson, the French Commissioner, but held them responsible for instance of fraud and accused them of turning blind eye.[29] Faced with such charges and threatened by the Parliament to sack them, the Commission resigned en masse on 16th March 1999.

Compared to the Commission, the Parliament has not much control over the Council. Apart from the Council's President presentation of his or her programme at the beginning of the Presidency and the account giving before the Parliament's Plenary during which the MEP are given the opportunity to question the Council President, contact between the two is very less.

3.5 The Court of Justice

The Court of Justice is supreme authority of the EU law. Its main purpose is to ensure the uniform application of the Union's law.

A feature of uniqueness of the EU among the international organization is that it incepts a legal order above that of its member states. There are two sources of EU law – primary and secondary law. The treaties constituted the primary law and are in effect integrated within the constitutional structure of the member states while the legislation enacted in the framework of the treaties constituted secondary.

The Court of Justice is composed of 15 (27) Judges, one each from each member-state and nine Advocates-General. They are chosen from persons with high integrity and possess the qualifications required for appointment to the highest judicial offices in their respective countries or who are jurisconsults of recognized competence by the member-states for renewable six years term.[30] To ensure continuity of office, the replacement of judges is done in such a way that every three years seven or eight judges are replaced alternately.

The judges select one of their members to be the President for three years renewable term. His tasks include overseeing the overall direction of the work of the Court by, for instance, assigning cases to the Court's Chambers, appointing judges, rapportuers to cases and setting schedule for cases.[31] He is also empowered, on application from a party, to order suspension of Union measures and to order such interim measures as he deems to be appropriate.[32]

The Court of Justice sits in plenary session of all the judges, or in chambers of either three or five or even seven judges. Plenary sessions are necessary if the cases involved member states or EU institutions or if the same requests so.

The judges are assisted by the nine Advocates-General who submit opinion on each of the cases heard by the Court. Article 116 of EC Treaty laid down the duty of the Advocates-General as 'acting with complete impartiality and independence, to make, in open Court, reasoned submission on cases brought before the Court of Justice.' In other words, the work of the Advocates-General is to make a thorough examination all of the aspects of the issue involved in a case, take account of all relevant law and then submit its opinion on the cases.

Powers and Responsibilities

The main task of the Court of Justice is to ensure that the law are observed directly or through the national Court or agencies. It is also responsible to rule on cases involving alleged infringement of the EU law, review the legality of actions and failure to act, and giving preliminary ruling on questions of the EU law in cases referred by national Court. In fulfilling its responsibilities the Court, however, cannot initiate action on its own. It should, either come through the Commission, national authorities or through legal action brought by individual and organizations whose interests are at stake.[33]

3.6 The European Court of Auditors

It is a taxpayers' representative, responsible for ensuring that the EU spent its funds according to its budgetary rules and regulations and for the purposes for which it is intended.[34] It came into being in 1977 replacing the earlier audit bodies of EEC and Eurotom and the ECSC and became full-fledge institution in 1993 under the Treaty of European Union.[35]

The Court of Auditors comprised of 15 (now 27) members, one each from each member-states. They are appointed for six years renewable term by a unanimous vote of the Council of Ministers. The nomination, however, is done by member states in consultation with the EP. The EP has the right to reject nomination but its decision is not binding on the Council. The members are chosen from person with high integrity and independent from state influence while performing their duties. They must belong to/have belonged to, an external audit body in their own country or be a person who are appropriately qualified in some other capacity.[36]

The members elect one of their members to be the President of the Court, for three years renewable term. The President's task is to ensure the smooth functioning of the Court as well as to represents it in its external relations.

Members are assigned a specific sector of activity for which they hold a particular responsibility regarding the preparation and implementation of the decision of the Court. Each sector fall under one of the three audit groups, which act primarily as coordinating agencies and fitters for plenary sessions of the whole Court. All-important decisions are taken in plenaries by majority vote if need be.

The task of the Auditors is to check whether all receipts and expenditures are in lawful and regular manner and whether financial management has been sound. In doing this, it does not have to wait for the end of the financial year and whenever necessary, is done on the spots. It also has to submit its observation on specific questions and deliver opinion at the request of one of the institutions and assist the Parliament in discharging their power of control over the implementation of the budget.

3.7 Decision-making Procedures and Types of Voting

European Union legislation is the core of the decision-making procedure. It can be distinctly divided into three different stages:

1. Initiative
2. Consultative, and
3. Decision-making

Initiating proposal is the first stage of decision-making. It is done by the Commission. The Parliament consult the public opinion through several advisory committees and it also takes into account the position of the political forces represented and then produces opinions in the form of resolution. The Council acts as the final decision maker.

There are several procedures which are involved in decision-making process. They are:

Consultative Procedures:

Under this procedure, the Council takes into consideration the Parliament's position on Commission's proposal, before it makes the final decisions. This procedure involves only one reading in the Parliament and the position or opinion of the Parliament is not binding. In case of non-adoption of the Parliament's opinion both the Commission and the Council has to give an explanation to the Parliament.

The following sequence of events takes place during Consultative procedure[37]:

a) The Council transmits the Commission's proposals to Parliament for an opinion.

b) The President of Parliament refers the proposals to the Committee responsible and where appropriate to any committees which must also be consulted for their opinion.

c) The committees conclusions are presented to the full house in the form of report.

d) The proposal is either approved or reject with or without amendments.

e) The Parliament's opinion is then sent to the Council and Commission so that the latter can if necessary; revise its original proposal in line with Parliament suggestion.

f) Finally the Council adopts the Community Act by majority and weighted majority as prescribed.

Cooperation Procedure

Introduced by the SEA, this procedure allows Parliament to improve proposed legislation by amendment through two readings. As before, the Commission makes a proposal and the Parliament adopts a position on it. At the first reading stage the Council examines the proposal and drafts a common position which is referred back to the Parliament with an explanation. If the Parliament is not satisfied, it can either reject or prepare amendment, within three months by an absolute majority of its component member. To act on the second reading the Council requires unanimous vote and puts the Parliament at an advantage as it can put pressure on the Council to take its view seriously. This procedure applies in European Regional Development Fund, Research, the

Environment and Overseas Cooperation and Development etc.

Co-decision Procedures

Under this procedure the Council and the Parliament share decision-making power equally. This procedure is built in around the possibility of third reading in the Parliament. The procedure is similar with the cooperation procedure but goes beyond it in two important aspects. Firstly, in the event of difference of opinion between the Council and the Parliament a Conciliation Committee is convened. Secondly, if the Conciliation Committee is not unable to resolve the differences and if the Council wants to press ahead, the Parliament can act on the basis of support of a qualified majority. If the Conciliation Committee is able to resolve the differences, the legislation is adopted in the name of the Parliament and the Council. This procedure applies to the free movement of workers, consumer protection, education, culture, health, trans-European Network.

Assent Procedure

This procedure is used, above all, for Constitutional act which shapes the identity and the structure of the European Union such as accession of new member, for association agreements, conclusion of important international agreement and the establishment of uniform procedure for elections to the Parliament.[38]

Special Procedures

These are mainly concerned with the establishment of budget, the financial provision governing the Communities' own resources and the procedures for amending treaties.

3.8 Types of Voting

Voting can be of three types:

a) *Simple majority*—which consists of an absolute

majority of the members of the Council, the Commission or the Parliament. This kind of vote is used to reject a proposal, by Parliament using cooperative procedure.

b) *Qualified majority*—under this voting system the 15 member state governments have a cumulative value of 87. Value of a vote in the Council is determined according to the size of member country. A minimum 62 out of 87 votes constitute a qualified majority. This principle of qualified voting ensures that the five larger states cannot outvote the smaller ten and the two larger states cannot by themselves constitute a blocking minority. The votes of the member states are weighted as follows[39]

EU-15

Germany	10
France	10
Italy	10
The UK	10
Spain	8
Belgium	5
Greece	5
The Netherlands	5
Portugal	5
Austria	4
Finland	4
Sweden	4
Ireland	3
Denmark	3
Luxembourg	2

c) *Unanimity*—Applied on issues, which are of vital interest to the member-states. This includes taxation, industry, culture, regional and social funds and the framework programme for research and technology

The Community law adopted by the Council or the Council and the Parliament jointly may take the following forms:[40]

Regulation: those laws which are directly applied without the need for national measures to implement them.

Directives: binds the member-states as to the objective to be achieved while leaving the national authority the powers to choose the form and means to be used.

Decision: are binding in all their aspects upon those whom they are addressed; and

Recommendation and opinion: which are not binding and it is in the hands of the member states whether to follow it or not.

3.9 European Union's Bureaucracy

The European Commission is widely understood as the executive body of the European Community, even though there is nothing in the original treaties to suggest the Commission should have the exclusive right to manage Community/Union policy. In fact, it was conferred upon the Council. The Council in turn conferred these powers to the Commission through secondary legislation. As such the Commission is required to exercise a wide range of executive function relating to the management, supervision and implementing of policies.[41]

The Commissioners elect a President from amongst themselves. The President has certain specific roles to perform. He has to represent the Commission within and outside the Community, provides a sense of direction to his fellow Commissioners and Commission as a whole oversees the Commission's administrative services and allocates policy portfolios to other Commissioners. Allocations of portfolios are usually very politicized with each member states demanding the most important and prestigious portfolios for their Commissioners.[42] The portfolios of the commissioners are as follows:

Romano Prodi: President (Italy).

Neil KIinnock: Vice-President (UK), Administrative Reforms.

Loyala De Palacio: Vice-President (Spain), Relation with the EP, Transport and Energy.

Mario Monti: (Italy) Competition.

Frits Boldestein: (the Netherlands), Internal Market, Taxation and Custom Union.

Chris Patten: (UK), External Relation.

Viviane Redding: (Luxembourg), Education and Culture.

Anna Diamanta Poulou: (Greece), Employment and Social Affairs.

Antonia Vitorino: (Portugal), Justice and Home Affair

Micheal Barnier: (France), Regional Policy.

Gunter Verheugen: (Germany), Enlargement.

Phillipe Busquin:(Belgium), Research.

Erkki Luikanen: (Finland), Enterprise, Information Society.

Poul Nielson: (Denmark), Development and Humanitarian Aid.

David Byrne: (Ireland), Health and Consumer Protection.

Margot Wallstrom: (Sweden), Environment

Micheal Schreyer: (Germany), Budget.

Pascal Lamy: (France), Trade.

Pedro Sikbes Mira: (Spain), Economic Monetary Affair.

Franz Fieschler: (Austria), Agriculture, Rural Development and Fisheries.

Though execution of EU's policy is the responsibilities of the Commissioners, it is the Commission's bureaucracies who are the real executors. Lying below the Commissioners, the Commission's bureaucracy is composed of European Civil Servants responsible for the day-to-day work. Popularly known as the "Eurocrats", they number around 1000 and are assisted by a similar number of technical and support staff.[43] It constitutes by far the biggest elements of the whole European Union's administrative framework, though it is tiny compared with the size of administration in the member-states.

The Commission staffs may be divided into two categories: permanent staff and temporary employees. The former is recruited through open examination, of which those of 'A' Grade, in particular are highly competitive.[44] While the temporary staff is recruited for a short period on contract basis. An internal career structure exists and most of the top jobs are filled by internal promotion.[45] However, practice of balance national representation at all level especially at 'Grade A' level often disturbed the meritocratic principles.

Organizationally, the Commission's bureaucracy is organized into 23 Directorate-Generals (DGs) and several Special Units and Services such as the Secretariat General, the Legal Services, the Statistic Office, etc. All the DGs are not same in size and importance which varies depending on the policy importance and workloads. Usually, the average DGs are divided into three to four divisions. In extreme case the DGs can have upto eight Directorates and 36 Divisions.

The Directorate-Generals are headed by Directors-General who report to the appropriate Commission or Commissioners dealing with the given policy area. Below the Directors-General are the Directors who head the Directorates while the heads of the Division heads the Divisions.

The administrative work of the Commission is provided by the Secretariat General of which the Secretary-General is the head. He is assisted by a number of deputies. The Secretariat General's task include control of legislative text, arranging Commission's agenda, distributing information to other institutions, coordination of functions, etc.

3.10 Council Secretariat

The Council has a separate General Secretariat which provided the main administrative support for the work of the Council. It has a staff of just over 2000, of which 200 are at 'A' Grade that is diplomatic level. It is situated in Brussels.

The Presidency of the Council rotates between the states every six months: January to June and July to December. The work of the President is to chair the Council meetings, convene meetings, either on his own initiatives or on the request of a member-state or the Commission, setting priorities and the objectives for the Council and consistency of policy development and representing the Council within and outside the Community.[46]

The main tasks of the Council Secretariat is to service the Council machinery from ministerial to working party levels by preparing draft agendas, keeping records, providing legal advice, processing and circulating decision and documentations, translating, and generally monitoring policy developments so as to provide an element of continuity and coordination in Council proceedings.[47] In exercising these responsibilities, the Secretariat works closely with representatives from the member-state of President-in-office.[48] However, the extent to which the President rely on the Council Secretariat varies considerably depending the size of the Country (smaller country relying more on the Secretariat) and on the member-state who hold the Council Presidency.

OTHER IMPORTANT ORGANS

Apart from the above five institutions, there are other institutions which are essential part of the EU working system

3.11 European Council

Before the 1974 Summit meet, the European Council was very few. In the Summit of 1974, it was decided to institutionalize the Summit meeting of the Heads of the States and Governments and in 1987 SEA, it was given the treaty base. The main reason for the creation of the European Council was a growing feeling that the Community was failing to respond adequately or quick enough to new and increasingly difficult challenges. This was so because of the decreasing power of the Commission after the Luxembourg Compromise and the inability to provide the necessary leadership by the Council of Ministers due to internal schism.

The membership is based on the Council of Ministers with a slight difference. Every member state is represented by the Head of the State and Foreign Minister. Apart from them another two members are selected from the Commission to participate at the negotiating meeting of the European Council. As such, there are 32 members of European Council-two each from each member states plus two from the Commission.[49]

The main tasks of the European Council are setting priorities, giving political direction, providing impetus for development and resolving contentious issues that have proved too difficult for the Council of Ministers. It does all these function at a general level though it sometimes deals with specific internal policy issues. The Maastricht Treaty further strengthened the power of the European Council by giving the overall development of policies of the second and third pillars of the Union under the general direction of this institution. This inevitably strengthened the position of the national governments in the EU system. The fact that decisions are taken on the basis of unanimous agreement add an extra inter-governmental element to the nature of EU.

3.12 European Investment Bank

This was established in 1958 under the Treaty of Rome with the aimed to promote economic and social cohesion by providing finance for public and private project in all economic sectors within and outside the Union. The bank is located in Luxembourg

All the 15 member-states are members of the Bank. It is manage by a Board of 15 Governors who are responsible for overseeing the bank's credit policy and meet once a year. Below the Board of Governors lies the Board of Directors consisting of 25 directors who are responsible for granting loans and guarantees, raising funds etc. Normally it meets every four to six weeks. The Managing Committee of the Bank looks after the day to day working of the Bank. The above three bodies are supported by the European Investment Bank administration which employed more than 800 staff.

3.13 The Economic and Social Committee

The Economic and Social Committee is a consultative body which comprises representatives of various types of economic and social activities. It is composed of 222 members appointed by the Council in consultation with the Commission. Membership allocation is broadly proportionate to size and population of the member-states.

EU-15

France	24
Germany	24
Italy	24
UK	24
Spain	21
Belgium	12
Greece	12
Netherlands	12
Portugal	12
Austria	11
Sweden	11
Denmark	9
Finland	9
Ireland	9
Luxembourg	6

To ensure the representation of a broad spectrum of interests and view, it is divided into three interest groups. The first group consists of Employer's group and is made up of representatives of employer's organization and Chambers of Commerce, the second made up of trade union representatives and the third group includes various interests' made up of representatives of farmer, small and medium size business etc. These are further divided into different section such as agriculture and fisheries, industry, commerce, etc.

The Committee elects a Chairman and a Bureau from amongst its members for a term of two years. The main function of the Chairman is to represent the Committee in relation with other EU institutions, member states and non-

EU organization and states.[50] The Bureau is made of 30 members and has a President, two Vice-Presidents and nine members from each group. They assist the Chairman in outside relation and are responsible for the general organization of the Committee's work.

It has an advisory power and the Council and the Commission are required to consult it where the treaty provides or where the two consider it appropriate.[51] It also has the right to issue on its initiatives.

3.14 Committee or Region

It is advisory body sets up under the treaty of EU to give regional and local authorities a bigger say in the legislative process. It is consistent with the principle of Subsidiarity, the most novel innovation of the Maastricht Treaty which means decisions should be taken as close as possible to the citizen. Since its first session in March 1994, it has emerged as a strong guardian of the principle.[52]

It consists of 222 members with a break up same as that of Economic and Social Committee. The members are appointed for a renewable four years term of office by the Council of Ministers.

It has an advisory power and the Council and the Commission are required to consult where the treaty provides or where the two considers such action appropriate.[53]

NOTES

1. John Pinder, "EC and Nation States: Case of Neo-federalism?", *International Affairs,* (London), Vol. 62, no.1, Winter 1985, p. 42.
2. Dr. Klaus-Dieter Borchardt, *"European Integration: Origin and Growth of EU",* (Luxembourg), 1995, p. 18.
3. Lee Miles and John Redmond, "Enlarging the European Union: the erosion of federalism?", *Cooperation and Conflict,* (Stockholm) Vol.31, 1999. p. 292.

4. Borchadt, *op.cit.*, p. 19.
5. *Ibid.* p. 20.
6. Neill Nugent, *The Government and Politics of European Union,* (London), 1995, p. 35.
7. Lee Miles, *op.cit.*, p. 301.
8. Richard Rose and Christian Haerpfer, "Democracy and enlarging the EU eastward, *Journal of Common Market Studies,* (Stockholm), Vol.33, n. 3, p. 444.
9. Lee Miles, *op.cit.*, p. 299.
10. Nugent, *op.cit.*, p. 127.
11. *Ibid.*
12. Council Guide, vol.I (Luxembourg) 1997, p. 15.
13. S.F. Goodman, *The European Union,* 3rd edition (London), 1996, p. 80.
14. Article 160, EC Treaty.
15. Geoffery and David Spence edition, *The European Commission,* (London), 1994, p. 43.
16. Nugent, *op.cit.*, p. 89.
17. Jo Shaw, *The Law of the European Union,* (London, 1996), p. 114.
18. Spence, *op.cit.*, p. 122.
19. Michelle Cini, *The European Commission: Leadership, Organization and Culture in the EU Administration,* (Manchester) 1999, p. 27.
20. Asian Age, 18th March 1999.
21. Nugent, *op.cit.*, p. 20.
22. Elaborated separately in the present chapter.
23. Martin Westlake, *A Modern Guide to the European Parliament* (London), 1994, p. 190.
24. Shaw, *op.cit.*, p. 35.
25. These terms are explained later in this same chapter.
26. Serving the EU: A citizen's guide to the institutions of the EU (Luxembourg), 1996, p. 6.
27. *The Times of India*, 17th March, 1999, New Delhi.
28. Article 167, EC Treaty.

29. Nugent, *op.cit.*, p.22.
30. *Ibid.*
31. Article 169-186, EC Treaty
32. Serving the European Union, n.26, p.36
33. Article 4, EC Treaty.
34. Nugent, *op.cit.*, p.249.
35. Werner Weidenfeld and Wolfgang Wessels, *Europe from A to Z: Guide to European Integration,* (Italy), 1996, p. 63.
36. *Ibid,* p. 66.
37. Shaw, *op.cit.*, p. 120.
38. Serving the European Union, n.26, p. 11.
39. All these are discussed under the function and power of the Commission.
40. Shaw, *op.cit.*, p. 111.
41. *Ibid.*
42. Nugent, *op.cit.*, p. 90.
43. *Ibid*
44. *Ibid*, p. 128.
45. *Ibid*, p.133.
46. *Ibid*, p. 134.
47. *Ibid*, p. 157.
48. *Ibid*, p. 237.
49. Shaw, *op.cit.*,, p. 130.
50. Serving the European Union, n. 26, p. 36.
51. Article 198c of the EC Treaty.
52. Nugent, *op.cit.*, p.232.
53. Article 179, EC Treaty.

4

RESPONSES TO NEEDS

Within and Outside-I

While the previous chapter was devoted to the functional, structural and procedural aspects of the EU, an attempt will be made, in the present and next chapters, to discuss the EU's responses to the changing needs within and outside the Union, substantiate the analysis with six features in particular – Common Agricultural Policy, Economic and Monetary Union and its relationship with the ACP countries, the US, India and Japan.

The origins of the EU's policies may be traced to a number of sources ranging from economic realities and opportunities, political imperatives to visionary leadership. For instances, the CAP was created to fight the evil of food shortage which had plagued Europe for more than one decade, while the EMU was established under the ingenious leadership of Jacques Delors.

4.1 The Common Agricultural Policy (CAP)

The Common Agricultural Policy is remarkedly complex assembly of instruments and regulations covering trade controls, price support measure, income transfers, production subsidies, health regulation, etc. Formulated in 1962 under the provision of Rome Treaty, CAP has been adapting to changing political and economic circumstances. From being a system which aimed at securing sufficiency in food supply, it has incorporated lately new areas of policy such as environmental protection, regional and rural development, consumer issues as well as managing the agricultural market in EU.

Objectives and the Working of CAP

CAP was created against an immediate backdrop of post-war food shortage. Securing sufficiency in food supply was the top priority of the policy makers. This was reflected in the objectives laid down for CAP, which are as follows:

(i) To increase agricultural productivity,

(ii) To give farmers a comparable standard of living,

(iii) To stabilize markets,

(iv) To guarantee food security and

(v) To provide food to consumers at reasonable prices.

The CAP was based on, and still remains so, three guiding principles set up by the specially convened conference of the Council of Ministers held at Stressa in 1958.

1. **Market Unity**: Creation of single market for all agricultural products based on common prices which are three fold: (a) Threshold price—the minimum price at which import product is sold inside the Community/Union; (b) Target price – the price which the farmers hope to get in domestic market; and (c) intervention prices—the price at which the Community/Union agencies stand ready to buy the surplus product.[1]

2. **Community Preference**: This principle seeks to promote Community/Union agricultural products over import from outside the Union. It takes the form of variable levies, custom duties, import duties and granting of export refund

as subsidies for EU producers wishing to export agricultural products.

3. **Financial Solidarity**: Under this principle, the CAP is financed by EU budget. The funding is done through the European Agricultural Guidance and Guarantee Fund (EAGGF), which have two sections—Guarantee section and Guidance section. The former section finances markets and prices and the latter, the structural policy.

CAP is implemented through 'Common Market Organisations' (CMO), which covers more than 90 per cent of the Community agricultural production. The CMO is charged, in particular with regulating prices, assistance in productions and marketing and the stabilization of import and export, popularly known as 'price support system'. The price support system is the mainstay of the CMO. In implementing the price system, the CMO followed certain basic rules.[2] It began with the setting of target price and the threshold price at the harvest times. The Community prices are usually set above the world market prices and are maintained in part by protective measures in the form of import levies, export subsidies, etc. When the Union prices fall due to excess supply, a minimum fixed price—known as the intervention price is fixed at which the Union must buy the surpluses. However, if the producers preferred to export the surpluses, they were given export subsidies to bridge the price gap between the Union and the world market. The Council establishes all prices applicable within the CAP annually and the costs are borne by the Guarantee section of EAGGF. This system of Constitutional prices has ensured that producers always had an outlet for their products; this in turn encouraged the farmer to produce more.

The CAP could be termed a success, especially, in realizing its objectives. Since the implementation of the CAP, Europe once a major importer of foodstuff has become not only self-sufficient but also an exporter of the same. The price support system has sustained farm incomes and a single market has been established for almost all the agricultural products. However, the very success of CAP in achieving its objectives revealed a number of deficiencies as the Union moved into surplus in most of its agricultural products. Some of the deficiencies/shortcomings are listed below:[3]

1. The prices and guarantee provided through intervention and production aid stimulated output at a rate increasingly beyond the market absorption capacity that, in turn led to a costly build up of stock.

2. The existence of price support system stimulated production growth and encouraged intensification of production technique, which have an adverse social and environmental effect.

3. The benefits of CAP offered by income support for farmers were very uneven depending almost exclusively on price guarantee; income support is largely proportionate to the volume of production. It, therefore, tended to favour large farmer while ignoring the vast majority of small and medium size family farms.

4. No improvement in per capita purchasing power of the farmer, nor was there much decline in number of people engaged in farming over the years.

5. The increasing growth of Guarantee section expenditure becomes a major source of crisis within the Union.

Apart from the shortcomings, the CAP also has experienced problems which are socio-economic in nature. Firstly, over half of the Union's farmers are above 55 yrs of age. Secondly, there are vast differences in income level between member states—the best placed having three times the per capita income of the least favoured. Thirdly, one in three farmers works part-time and lastly, there is a significant difference in the size of holding per member state.[4]

In the light of the above listed shortcomings, the CAP as applied is no longer in a position to achieve its objectives. The mechanism was created at a time of food shortage with an aim to meet the situation. In a situation where there is good sufficiency and even surpluses, this becomes outdated and needs to be replaced. The result was the reform procedure, which began as early as 1968 and of which the 1992 reform package was the most radical of all.

Reforming CAP

The need for reforming CAP has been felt as early as the 1960s accompanied by discussion on reform proposals. The general objectives of reform at that time was to rein back price support and promote structural adjustment in order to curb industry's propensity for excess production as well as increasing expenditure on CAP. The first such proposal was the 'Mansholt Plan'. It advocated a more prudent price policy and improved structural reform to avoid problems of surpluses and rising expenditure.[5]

The plan did not materialize because of the stiff opposition by the Community farming circle. In the 1970s several measures were introduced which were designed to encourage domestic consumption including subsidies to certain categories of final consumers, subsidies to industrial user of food products and even 'denaturing premiums' to encourage the use of grain in the livestock feed.[6] Attempts were also made to decrease the budgetary cost of the existing instrument, intervention buying by manipulating its rule of policy. The measures, however, were not effective enough to curb both the increasing budget and the excess production.

In the 1980s, further steps were taken to contain the budgetary pressures and excess production. The efforts saw the introduction of new supply control mechanisms: budgetary stabilizer, market quotas and co-responsibility levies.

Budgetary stabilizer—was introduced to contain the budgetary crisis caused by over-spending on agricultural market support. It is a mechanism which reduced market support when output rose beyond specified threshold level, together with measures to promote structural changes in agriculture which would reduce excess production.[7] The system specified Maximum Guarantee Quantities for each product for which price support was guaranteed but beyond which there is cut in price or subsidies. The key element of this mechanism was the financial support for 'set aside scheme' – which provides financial compensation for farmers who withdrew some part of land out of production;

Extensification—with reduction in output per hectare of 20%; 'production conversion' scheme for diversification into products not subject to surplus; and early retirement for farmers—with their farmland either used to enlarge other farms or assigned to non agricultural uses.[8]

Co-responsibility levies—these concern producers marketing tax which are applied to every producer irrespectively but is refunded to those whose output does not exceed the Maximum Guarantee Quantities.

Marketing Quotas—It is a maximum quota imposed on Community producers beyond which a very high tax or levy is charged. It has been a feature of the sugar regime since its inception in the 1960s and then extended to milk product in 1984. Initially each state was allocated national quotas or reference quantity set equal to their 1981 delivery levels plus one percent which were then allocated to individual farmers, again on the basis of their historical production levels.[9]

Despite the introduction of such on elaborate supply control mechanism, there was no relief from the mounting surplus and the over expenditure in agriculture. In fact, there was an increase in the stockpile of cereal and beef by 150 and 70 percent respectively. The call for reform intensified and resulted in the 1992 CAP reform.

As mentioned earlier, the 1992 reform was the most radical of all the CAP reforms. It was necessitated by two pressures: internal and external pressures. Internal pressures stemmed from increasing stocks and budget expenditure that had an adverse effect on consumers, environment and overall budget of the Community/EU. While external pressures were expressed through the Uruguay Round of GATT that linked reform of CAP, a major cause of trade distortion upto 1990, to obtaining agreement on GATT.

The most important feature of the Mc-Sharry Reform Package was the shift from price support to direct support for farmers' income; setting aside of land from agricultural production and the introduction of three measures to accompany the reform: the agri-environment and afforestation schemes and an improved early retirement schemes for farmers aged over 55.[10]

Its aim was to bring better balance between supply and demand in the internal market. It did so by phased reduction in the target price and, hence the threshold and intervention prices of cereal and animal products, thus bringing them closer to those in the world market. The loss in the income was compensated with a series of direct aid to farmers. The direct payment was linked with the obligation to set aside, under which each cereal farmer producing more than 92 tones has the option either to produce the same quantity and sell at the market price or set aside part of his arable land and get compensatory payment in addition to his market returns for output from land remaining in production.

In the case of animal products, aid was paid per head in the livestock sector. Known as 'Premium', the compensations are payable where animal densities on open grazing land are below prescribed level i.e. 3.5 LU/ha (livestock unit per hectare) at 1993 level.[11]

Another element of the reformed package is in relation to the 'accompanying measures'. These include an improved early retirement scheme with a purpose to provide income for farmers who decide to retire, to improve the viability of agricultural holdings and to reassign farmlands that are viable to non-agricultural uses; and two new schemes to encourage less extensive forms of production. They are more environmental friendly farming and the development of afforestation of marginal land. Under these schemes financial assistance is provided to farmers who undertake to (a) reduce the fertilizer usage, (b) change or maintain extensive production methods, (c) reduce the number of sheep or cattle per hectare, (d) use production method compatible with the natural resources and maintenance of the countryside, (e) rear local breed in danger of extinction, (f) ensure the upkeep of abandoned farm or woodland, (g) set aside farmland for environmental purposes for at least 20 years, and (h) manage land for public access and leisure activities.[12] The funding of these schemes which was under the Agricultural Structure Policy was switched to Guarantee section of the EAGGF as a part of the reform package.

In brief, 1992 CAP reform was a response to the adverse effect and pressure created by the past policies. It was a way to reduce subsidized export and internal price support system through introduction of series of new mechanisms to help more market oriented production. It also marked the shift of emphasis from that of securing self-sufficiency in food towards securing environmental friendly production while retaining its original principles.

Since the reform, there has been a considerable improvement of market balance and a decrease of livestock in most of the reformed sectors. The per capita income of farmer also saw upward trend. This was affected by the improved market situation, the strong adaptation capacity of farmers, the agri-monetary content and last but not the least, the continuing decline in agricultural employment.[13] The reduction of price support and the introduction of direct payments have benefited consumers as part of the burden of agricultural support has shifted away from them. The positive impact includes the more rational use of fertilizers and pesticides, incentives for a long term improvement in the territorial distribution of livestock rearing etc. Its negative aspects are mainly the encouragement given to irrigate crops through regionalization of direct payment to cereals, oil seeds, protein crops, as well as the relative advantage given to intensive livestock farming through lower feed prices and subsidizing silage.[14] Encouraged by such a success, the Commission in 1995 December proposed 'deepening and extending the 1992 reform through further shift from price support to direct payment, and developing a coherent rural policy to accompany this process.[15]

Thus CAP since its inception has been adapting to changing political and economic circumstances. At the time of its inception securing self-sufficiency and helping the farmers' production were the key concerns. However, with the realization of these objectives and the subsequent overproduction, appropriate reforms were undertaken to curb the problem. The most radical which was the 1992 CAP reform culminated as a result of pressure from both within and outside the Union.

4.2 The Economic and Monetary Union (EMU)

The Economic and Monetary Union (EMU) means a single monetary policy within a single market with a single currency. This concept was introduced into the European Community Treaty by the Maastricht Treaty. The main objective of EMU is price stability which the member states hope to achieve by giving up all power to use monetary policy to stabilize their economies.

The inspiration for currency stability in Europe has deep roots. Some came from the 19th century, for example, the Latin Monetary Union, Germany Currency Union, Gold Standard etc. However, when the EC was established in the late 1950s, monetary union was not explicitly on the agenda, although exchange rate was identified as a matter of common interest. This was because the Brettonwoods system was still in good shape and exchange rates were fixed against US dollar. It was only in the early 1970s that the Community started seriously to consider the need for a monetary union. The impetus for this comes from both within and outside the community. The outside impetus was provided by the collapse of Brettonwoods system and Nixon's abandonment in 1971 of the link between gold and dollar while the coalesce together of France and Germany so as to move out of the traditional grooves of chauvinistic pride and prejudice to shape up a new European Vision provide impetus to European integration in the monetary field.

At the same time, the Community was facing a major challenge. The imminent enlargement of the original six members to include, Denmark, Ireland, the UK and Norway which could stagnate the integration process. To meet this challenge, the 1969 Summit decided to create EMU. The task of investigating the possibilities and proposing recommendation was entrusted to an expert working committee under the chair of Luxembourg Prime Minister, Pierre Werner.[16] Known as the Werner Report, the report defined EMU as "comprising irrevocable convertibility of member states' currencies, free movement of capital, and the permanent locking of exchange rate, the replacement of the member states' currencies by a single currency".[17] This was to be achieved by 1980.

The plan could not materialize because it involved too much sacrifice of sovereignty on the part of the member states which they were not willing to do so at that stage and also because of the deteriorating economic condition caused by the collapse of Brettonwoods system, 1973 oil crisis and the depression. The report was later used as a basis for Delors Report 1989, leading to the creation of EMU.

Undeterred, the Community soon introduced a system to tie the currencies to the Deutschmark, dubbed "the snake in the tunnel". The range of fluctuation between their currencies was restricted to a band of ± 2.25 per cent. This was joined, apart from the original six, by the UK, Norway, Ireland and Denmark.[18] However, the snake was destined to lead a fitful and unsatisfactory life. Britain joined in May 1972, only to leave six weeks later, and both France and Italy joined and left twice.

The European Monetary System (EMS)

The continuous search for 'monetary stability' within European Community led to the creation of European Monetary System (EMS) in 1979. The EMS marked a major shift from the earlier method including the snake. It was more of an institutional and procedural mechanism to create a zone of monetary stability.[19] In other words the EMS was not designed to bring about the EMU, it was a mechanism which aimed at facilitating closer cooperation between states and thereby ensuring a stable monetary environment within and between the EC members which could act as a phase of transition.[20]

The EMS has three main elements.[21] They are:

1. The European Community Currency Unit (the ECU);
2. The European Monetary Cooperation Fund (EMCF); and
3. The Exchange Rate Mechanism (ERM).

The ECU is a monetary unit based on a basket of all EC currencies. The number of units of each currency in the ECU is fixed; the weights of the various currencies change over time, as intra European exchange rates fluctuate. It would act as the numeraire for the ERM and the unit of account of all the EC transactions.

The ERM is the centerpiece of EMS. It acted as a parities grid, where the exchange rates of the national currencies are irrevocably tied together within a nominated central and a permissible band of fluctuation. Upto 1993, the permitted fluctuation band was ± 6 per cent, arranged for its transitional period.[22] The Central rates are fixed and revised only with realignment by mutual agreement of the states participating in the ERM together with the Commission. The ratios of one country's central rate to another's form the bicentral rate.

The European Monetary Cooperation Fund (EMCF) was established to provide very short term, short term and medium term credit to ease any temporary balance of payment difficulties. It acts as a pool for approximately 20 per cent of the participating gold and dollar reserves, in exchange for which members would receive ECU deposits in order to settle internal debts arising from intervention over exchange rate fluctuations.[23]

Although EMS includes all member states, not all members participated in the ERM. The UK had not joined in the ERM until 1992 while Greece was never a member. The introduction to the ERM, nevertheless, helped to stabilize the participants' exchange rate. Despite the intermittent adjustments and 13 realignments including the 1992 realignment, there has been a sharp decrease of exchange rate volatility since the inception of EMS. Not only this, the inflation rate between the participating EMS members declined since 1979 along with it the inflation differential between participating members has also been eroded.[24]

The increasing stability of exchange rate signified an evolution of the ERM into an economic policy instrument, as its members sought economic convergence with low level of inflation. The ability to stabilize variation in exchange rate is one of the most successful aspects of the system.

The success of ERM in stabilizing exchange rate and converging policies offered a basis for the renewed efforts, which began in the late 1980s to move by stages to a single currency or to the permanent locking of exchange rate. This move was further facilitated by the creation of Single European Market which was completed in 1992.

1992 EMS Crisis

Despite the existence of ECU as the numeraire for the ERM, the Deutschmark came to play an important role, being the best inflation performer within the ERM. It was against the Deutschmark that the other ERM members used the fixed exchange rate to increase their anti-inflationary credibility. Germany became the main anchor of ERM and whatever policy the German independent Central Bank adopted became the ERM policy, as the other member follows the German example in order to limit the growth in their money supply so as to balance their inflationary rates with Germany. This system was under serious strain, when Germany, after its Unification decided against revaluation of the Deutschmark. The resultant inflationary pressure was met by raising the interest rate to higher level. This precipitated instability in the ERM, as other participants had to raise their own interest rate in order to maintain their exchange rates within the prescribed band.[25]

The instability was seriously compounded by the activities of the speculators which spread a rumour of imminent currency devaluation which cause a frenzied activity of buying and selling currencies. The political uncertainty surrounding the referenda on Maastricht acted as an immediate triggering point of the 1992 EMS crisis.

The Danish rejection and the French hesitation in signing the Maastricht Treaty and the resultant strengthening of the Deutschmark put considerable pressure on Lira and Sterling. Unable to maintain their exchange within the prescribed band, they left ERM in September 1992. The other ERM participants were not far behind. Spain, Portugal and Ireland devalued their currencies. Even the French franc came under intense pressure but was beaten off by a combined defense operation mounted by French and German banks. The crisis continued through most part of 1993. Devaluation of currencies persists despite substantial intervention by the Central banks. Except for the Dutch guilder, there were no currencies, which were not touched by the crisis. As a result the fluctuation band was widen to $\pm$ 15 per cent of either side of the central rate on 2nd August 1993 and thus saved the system from collapsing. Only the Netherlands chose to retain the original $\pm$ 2.25 percent band against Deutschmark.

Towards the Economic and Monetary Union

The renewed efforts to create single currency or the permanent locking of exchange rate between the Community member states which began in the late 1988, culminated in the adoption of single currency "Euro" on 1st January 1999 by eleven member states of the EU. After the completion of the Single European Market, this is a logical step which would eventually lead to the political Union of Europeans. The EMU provision as laid down in the Maastricht Treaty has set out the constitution for the Central Bank of the Union, a time-table for the approach to full Union and a set of criteria or fitness condition for membership to the Union.[26]

The single currency would have two major benefits.[27]

1. It would eliminate the barriers not only of trade, but also of capitals flows and the movement of people across

natural frontier association with separate national currencies within the single market.

2. It is the ultimate solution to problem arising from ERM instability between the currencies of member states.

The time-table for approach to full EMU set three stages. The first stage began on 1st July 1990. The objective of the stage was to increase monetary coordination, to bring all member-states into EMS, to complete the Single European Market and to carry out amendment that would later be necessary.[28] The second stage started on 1st January 1994, with the commencement of work by the European Monetary Institute (EMI). The main job of the EMI was to study the requirements of the European Central Bank, which would have executive powers in the stage three of EMU, when single currency replace the individual national currencies of the participating countries. The third stage commenced on 1st January 1999 on the basis of the majority countries who satisfied the 'Convergence Criteria'.

The convergence criteria which were laid down by the Maastricht Treaty are as follows:

1. Inflation rate should not be more than one and half percent point higher than the average of the best performing states.
2. Long-term interest rates not to exceed more than 2 points above the same bench mark.
3. Budget deficit should not exceed 3 per cent of GDP
4. Public debt not to be more than 60 per cent of the GDP, and
5. Exchange rate should be within the normal margins of the ERM for 2 years.

Before embarking on the third stage all the member countries, which want to participate, have to meet these criteria. However, given the financial turbulence caused by the ERM crisis, only one state, Luxembourg, was able to comply with all the criteria by the end of 1996. As a result, in actual practice, the criteria were loosely applied. For instance, public debt criterion was deemed met if the ratio was sufficiently diminishing and so on. Using such a flexible convergence criteria 11 European Union countries were listed qualified to join the single currency in 1998.

Thus, on 1st January 1999, 11 member-states out of 15 adopted common single currency "Euro" marking the beginning of the third stage and hence the EMU. This constitutes a landmark in the annals of European integration because it proof the determination of the member-states, not withstanding manifold obstacles and constraints, to move ahead in deepening as well as widening its regional integration. However, four countries—the UK, Denmark, Sweden and Greece did not participate. The first three were unwilling to surrender their financial autonomy. The UK apart from its unwillingness to surrender her financial autonomy, her own economy and unemployment level was in better shape than that of the EU at that time. Greece, though it would have loved to join the bandwagon, did not meet the convergence criteria.

As plan, on 1st January 2002, the actual notes and coins of the new Euro came into circulation replacing the existing currencies. This laid the groundwork for further steps towards European Integration. But, whether EMU is a major step on the road to a United States of Europe as implied in the new year eve speech of the French President the "the Euro will change Europe[29] and above all people's mentality on a mere strengthening of the existing economic union" remains to be seen.

4.3 The Lome Conventions

Lome regime is one of the most long-lived and comprehensive arrangements in North- South relations. It is an economic treaties which linked the EU with 70 developing African, Caribbean and Pacific (ACP) states[30] to promote and expedite the socio-economic and cultural development of the ACP states. This is a unique phenomenon in a largely dispiriting saga of North-South relations started way back in 1975, with the signing of the treaty in Lome, the capital of Logo for a period of five years. The successive treaties are called Lome Conventions. Since then four Lome Conventions had been signed, the last is in 1990, which ran upto the year 2000.

Lome Convention developed from earlier agreement between the EEC and the colonies of the European states that had joined the EEC. It was the outcome of the French insistence to pursue its colonial link at the Community level. Consequently, the Treaty of Rome devoted a chapter called 'Association of the Overseas Countries and Territories' in which the nature of the Community in relationship with the colonies and ex-colonies of not only France but also of Italy and Belgium were laid down.[31] Its main objective was "the promotion of the economic and social development of the countries and territories and to establish close economic relationship between them and the Community.[32] The task was entrusted to the Implementing Convention functional for five years. This was to achieve through Preferential trade which was to be reciprocal in nature; abolition of custom duties on goods imported from Associate Countries, though the latter can levy duties for development purpose and through the creation of Economic Development Fund (EDF) to offer grants plus assistance and aid to the Associate.[33]

However, by 1960s with most of the colonies getting independence, the term of ECs relations with ACP countries need some alteration. The result was the Yaounde Convention 1965, which regulated trade and cooperation, between EC and the former colonies of France, Italy, and Belgium without changing the basic tenets. This was followed by second convention with only one innovative feature, i.e the introduction of Joint Association of African and Malagsy states[34] (AAMS) and the EEC composing of the Council of Ministers, Parliamentary Conference and a Court, that not only provided a valuable seat for learning but also act as a major decision maker.[35]

Again in 1970s a complete revision of the Community's economic relations with the developing countries was made necessary by three factors—the accession of Britain, Denmark, and Ireland in 1973; the call for 'New International Economic Order' by developing countries in order to restructure global economic relations along a more equitable lines; and the oil crisis.

At the time of the negotiation for its accession, Britain had negotiated for pursuing her relations with the Commonwealth States at the Community level. The outcome of those negotiations was the Lome I Convention signed at Lome, the capital of Togo, in 1975. The Convention a much enlarge group of developing countries from African, Caribbean and Pacific, 40 states at the time of signing but now increased to include other 30 states. Except for Ethiopia and Liberia all these states were the colonies of one of the EU member states.

The purpose of the Lome Convention did not deviate from the earlier Conventions, i.e, to promote and expedite the economic and social development of the ACP states, and to consolidate and diversify their relation in the spirit of solidarity and mutual interest. What differentiates the Lome was the manner in which the objective is to be pursued. Under the term of the Lome, the EU guaranteed the ACP states

'Privileged Commercial Relations' but without the earlier system of reciprocality. In other words, the ACP states were given free access to the EU market for 99 percent of its products without any obligation to offer the same to EU. The amount of EDF was substantially increased and the European Investment Bank gave loans for national and regional development programme.

The other novel aspects of Lome Convention was introduction of "STABEX", a scheme designed to compensate ACP claimants for unavoidable decline in their export earning from agricultural goods in the EU; SYMIN, (introduced in the Lome II) a similar scheme for ACP mineral exporters; and a Centre for Industrial Development (CDI) which was charged with the task of assisting ACP states industrial development.[36]

As for its institution the Lome Convention adopted institutional procedures begun under the Yaounde Convention with a minor changes to form a joint Council of Ministers, Joint Committee of Ambassadors and Joint Consultative Assembly.[37] A permanent Secretariat was also created.[38]

Despite such and elaborate arrangement, the Lome Convention did not escape criticism. Some of which are:[39] (1) there was no overall increase in the ACP export to EU except for high oil export, (2) the STABEX was under-financed and the product incorporated was narrowed down to agricultural product only and, (3) the CDI was made inadequately financed to make any substantial impact on ACP industrialization.

All these drawbacks, however, were covered by the availability of the unconditional aid and grant on generous term and further agreements were signed albeit lack of enthusiasm. In 1980 Lome II, 1985 Lome III and 1990 Lome IV. There was not much change in the Lome II and LomeIII.

But Lome IV saw a visible shift in the approach to EU-ACP relationship.

Lome IV saw a shift in the equation of EU-ACP relationship. For the first time Lome aids were made conditional on sensible economic and social policies, democratic decision making, adequate governmental transparency and accountability, creation of market friendly environment for development measures to combat corruption as well as respect for rule of law, human rights and freedom of press and expression.[40] This imposition of eligibility criteria was prompted by the growing EU disquiet that its aid was being misused by the ACP countries, the increasing economic problem faced by most of the African states, the Structural Adjustment Programme started by the World Bank and International Monetary Fund as a condition for obtaining loan and grants and the increasing engagement of the EU in the economic and political reconstruction of the Eastern and Central European Countries.

As such Lome IV emphasis on financial and technical support for structural adjustment which would help ACP states to continue economic reforms which were considered necessary. At the same time aiming to make the social consequences of such reform easy to bear, it also emphasized on the protection of the environment with a highlight on problems of resource detention and desertification and the rapidly growing population as well as on the regional economic development through the uses and coordination of Lome funds to encourage regional economic cooperation.

The Lome IV also made improvement on some of its mechanisms. STABEX payment were made non refundable while increasing the EU's control on the manner of spending. SYMIN were made available in grant form not only to ACP states but to mining companies as well. And lastly, the EDF was geared towards increasing its grant elements so as to rescue the African states from indebtedness. Lome IV also increased the duration of the Convention from 5 to 10 years with a provision for renewal of financial protocol after 5 years and strengthens the CDI.

As provided for by the Lome IV, negotiation for a mid-term renewal was held in June 1995. It saw the deepening of the conditionality imposed at the beginning of the Lome IV. The main feature was the extension of conditionality to all the EU's aid programmes and not just to structural adjustment facility. The new conditions includes observance of the principle of good governance and implementation of economic policies conducive to promote market economy and private sectors, transferring the responsibility for preparation and appraisal of projects and financial proposal away from ACP to EU.[41]

In this way, the EU policy towards the ACP states has been adapting according to the economic and political needs. At the time of its inception the main purpose of the Lome was to help in the development of the ACP states without any conditions attached. However, by the time of Lome IV, 25 years after the Lome I, conditionality has become the main stay of the Lome Convention. The shift may be explained in terms of ACP states failure to bring about any significant development in its economic and political situation despites the availability of huge amount of EU grants and aids and the shifting of EU development policies towards the new democratic countries of Eastern and Central European countries. This is evident from the fact that the EU aid which originally concentrated on ACP states have now mostly goes to these newly emerging democratic of Eastern and Central Europe which in turn is again used for developing market economy as well as democratic practices in these countries who all aspire to be a member of EU one day or the other.

4.4 Relationship with the US, Japan and India

With the US

The EU relation with the United States of America is marked by a complex interplay of cooperation, shared interest and conflict. The early days shows the dependent of EU on the US for both economic and political security. However, gradually this cooperation turned into conflict, especially in trading arrangement but without losing the sight of its shared interest totally.

Europe's relation with the US goes beyond the formation of the EU (earlier EC) the US had been a major contributor of fund for European economic recovery and reconstruction in the form of Marshall Plan. The NATO ties the two in political and security field. When the six founding members of the EU embarked on establishing economic community in the late 1950s the US was very supportive of the endeavour but also apprehensive about the implication of such a custom union on her own economy. The apprehension, however, was overridden in the context of her economic dominance and the need for European order.

The benign attitude of the US towards the EU started eroding gradually from the 1960s. The US began to feel the impact of the custom union especially, the over protectionist CAP which got manifested in the Chicken war 1963-1966. CAP form the major area of EU-US conflict. The US used the Kennedy Round GATT to try to blunt the effect of the EEC's policies through agreements to reduce the world tariff level but found the Community a though negotiator, that no deal was reached in the area.[42] The period saw a conflict in political and security field. The US refusals to share nuclear know how with France led to the withdrawal of France from NATO. This was compounded by the EEC's refusal to share the burden of security.

During the 1970s and 1980's the US attitude towards the EU became generally more hostile and began to see the latter as an important rival in the world market.

The 1970s was a period of economic stagnation and inflation for the US and also for other parts of the world. The depression caused by oil crisis was affecting the whole world. To cushion off this effect the US had devalued its dollars. In contrast, the EU was witnessing an economic boom of unprecedented nature. The success CAP in accomplishing its objectives and the subsequent surplus in agriculture contributed to economic growth within the Union. Ironically, CAP had instituted the prime dispute area between the two since the beginning. To counter the growth in the EU, the US took a series of unilateral actions that change the nature of world trade. One of which was the declaration of New Economic Policy, a unilateral response to US balance of payment problems and domestic difficulties, with EU as its main target. However, despite the existence of tension in the economic area, the two nevertheless made an effort to rededicate and renew the Atlantic partnership leading to Atlantic Declaration in the early 1970s.

The dispute between the two got more intensified in the 1980s. In the 1980s the US increasingly saw the EU as an economic superpower, a formidable economic power but which was impervious to the US demand. This image was strengthened by the SEA and the implementation of the Single Market.

There was mounting number of trade dispute between the two. The prime dispute was over CAP. The platform used for negotiating the CAP dispute was the Uruguay Round GATT. The US was supported by the Cairn Group.[43]

In the GATT negotiation table the US had demanded 90 percent cut in the export subsidies and 75 per cent in other support[44] but was offered 30 percent cut in subsidies backdated to 1986 by the EU.[45] Unable to reach an agreement the negotiation was suspended in December 1990. Finally, in 1993 an agreement was reached to reduce agricultural subsidies: price support by one-fifth and subsidized exports reduced in value by 36 percent and in volume by 21 percent. These reductions to be phased over six year were based on 1991-1992 levels.

Apart from trade dispute the American insistence on trying to link economic with political and security interests has also caused friction with the EU. Known as 'extra territorial problems' the famous example of such friction was the US embargo in 1982, on the use by European firms of some American goods, patent, and licence to build the Siberian pipeline.[46] The US had imposed sanctions on the pipeline in the aftermath of martial law in Poland seeing the pipeline as a threat to the independence of Europe. But the measure had to be withdrawn in the face of EU opposition.

The relationship between the EU and the US deteriorated further by the passing of Omnibus Trade Act which empowered US government to take action against those countries found using unfair trade practices. This was resented very much by the EU as it was seen as evidence of protectionism.

Thus, in 1980s the EU-US relations was marked by the former gaining upper hand in most of the major events, which revealed not only the EU's power to resistance but also the limitation of the American power to define its policy areas.

In the 1990s, the US image of the EU had become that of competitor. Most of the time they did not see eye to eye. The friction which crept in since the 1960s had worsened. The US reluctance to accord equal position also contributed more to the deteriorating conditions.[47]

a) the collapse of Soviet bloc

b) the failure to reach agreement in the Uruguay Round-GATT negotiation had posed substantial challenge to the continuation of multilateral trading system.

c) the crisis in the Gulf, followed by the collapse of Yugoslavia, has created the tension between the EU role as a civilian power and demand for political and military commitment.

These three plus the inclusion of more countries in the European Economic Area by EU by the end of the century also added friction.

However, despite the existence of such a great tension between the two, both are inter-dependent to each other. The trade between the two along with that of Japan constitutes more than half of the total world trade. As such, there is a continuous search for renewing of ties between the two based on recognition of their mutual dependence and respective strength.

With Japan

In contrast to EU-US relations, the EU-Japan relationship is purely economic and conducted in a climate of relative indifference. It is only in the recent years that the two have taken greater interest in each other.

The lack of contact in the early years of the EU's existence may be explained in terms of Japan over-dependence on US for almost everything -defence, market etc, and the fact that EU has no competence yet to negotiate any agreement outside the Community. All trading relations were conducted bilaterally. It was only in the 1970s that the EU attempted negotiation with Japan. However, Japan's restricted imports and financial assistance given to export combined with the EU's demand for a 'safeguard clause' against a sudden expansion of Japanese imports led to the breakdown of the trade negotiation in 1971.[48] Despite the existence of such a discouraging trend, a mutual exchange of permanent delegations was agreed in 1975 which, however, could not bring about better relationship.

The absolute efforts to negotiate an agreement with Japan in the early years were superimposed by the devaluation of dollar by US in 1971, the first oil crisis 1973 and the second in 1979. To counter the impact of such depression, Japan redoubled its export efforts and also depreciated Yen. This added to the trade surplus of Japan which has been persistent and growing at the expense of the other trading partners particularly,[49] the EU. The Europeans reacted with resentment out of fear which led to the gap between the two being more widened. Repeated attempts of the Commission to secure improved market access did not succeed.

In the 1980s, the EU-Japan relations dipped almost to non-existence. Trade confrontation was overriding the relations. The growth of Japanese exports cars and consumer electronics deepened the friction. The confrontation without conversation was evidence from torrential exports and closed domestic market on one side and existence of protectionist counter-measure on the other. The increasing dominance of Japanese exports in the European market, particularly automobile has led to the continuing hostility towards Japan.[50]

However, from the 1988 onwards, the EU-Japan relations have brightened up. This was facilitated by change in attitude on both sides. In the case of Japan, the new muscle the EU acquired through implementation of the Single Market[51] was the precipitating factor. In case of the EU, the change came in 1989, when the Council adopted a set of Conclusion on EU-Japan relations that significantly altered the way in which the EU approach Japan.[52]

The conclusions made by the 1992 Council contained two new elements of significance for the overall EU-Japan relations:

- Trade assessment mechanism (TAM) and the new industrial policy.[53] TAM has three purposes[54] (i) to put the selection of sectors to be examined on a more rational basis, (ii) to remove the systematically confrontational character inevitable in pursuit of an agenda fixed by industry alone: (iii) to put trade discussions on an explicitly objective and reciprocal basis.
- To provide a permanent meeting forum for the Japanese and the Europeans without the need for debilitating and protracted negotiation before agenda can be agreed and a meeting can be fixed.

The second new element is borne out of the increased Japanese investment in European soil.

The change in the EU approach was affected by the shift in the member states attitude towards Japan over the 1980s. Great Britain, one of the most anti-Japanese was one of the first to change its attitude towards Japan, "reckoning that Japanese were of greater benefit to the UK as a large-scale investors and would be grateful to the UK for supporting Japan in the EU".[55] This was manifested in the British welcoming attempts to establish car assembly plants by Japan in EU. Other members also slowly change tact. Even France, an obstinant oppositor of Japan, also changed its attitude toward Japan. Apart from trade, EU-Japan now includes subjects like science and technology, the environment and development aid.

EU-Japan relations were given further boast, albeit indirectly, by the end of the cold war. Closely at the heel of the EU-US declaration, EU-Japan made a declaration which introduced an annual meeting at Heads of the Government level to match the practice between US and the EU. The meeting, however, was inconclusive after two or three meetings.

Thus, the relationship between the EU and Japan which had begun in a state of relative indifferences has slowly graduated into a partner. There is still much room for improvement, especially in the political field. An EU-Japan relationship based on strong economic and political relationship could alter the existing world order, if the two can trust each other to form such an alliance.

With India

Unlike the US and Japan, the EU-India relation was started in a cordial conditions and keep on improving from being a purely economic to that of Strategic partners. India-Europe relations go beyond the formation of EU. Both have trade relations since the ancient time. Post-EC/EU-India relation started in the early 1960s. In fact India was amongst the first countries to establish diplomatic relation with EU, in 1962, then EEC. This was followed by the signing of a Commercial Cooperation Agreement in 1973 by the two which form the basis of bilateral relationship between India and EU till the two signed five year Commercial and Economic Cooperation Agreement in 1981. Post-1981 witnessed the establishment of EC Delegation in India and also the launching of EC-India Cooperation and Exchange Programme (EICEP) for exchange of faculty from management schools. Then the 1994 Co-operation Agreement on Partnership and Development, signed in 1993 with a wide-raging third generation agreement took the relationship between the two well beyond trade and economic cooperation.

The basis of this cooperation as stated in article 1 of the Cooperation Agreement was and still is, respect for human rights and democratic rights while the principle objective - to enhance and develop, through dialogue and partnership, the various aspects of cooperation between the two in order to achieve a closer and upgraded relationship.[56] The Agreement took the EU-India relations way beyond trade and economic cooperation and covers such areas as Environment, Science and Technology, Information and Culture, Human Resource Development, Drug abuse control, etc.

The Agreement also retain the Joint Commission set up under the 1981 Agreement on Commercial and Economic Cooperation, as the central guardian mechanism to oversee and inspire the entire range of cooperation activities between EU and India. Joint Commission is responsible for ensuring the proper functioning of any sectoral agreements concluded or may be concluded between the two. It is composed of representatives of both sides, at an appropriate high level. It meets every year alternately in Brussels and New Delhi on datė fix by mutual agreement. Extraordinary meetings can also be convened by agreement between the two. Under this Joint Commission, there are three sub-commissions on trade, economic cooperation; development cooperation, that cover a more detailed agenda and report directly to the Joint Commission.

The institutional basis for EU-India political dialogue is a *Joint Political Statement* signed simultaneously with the third generation Co-operation Agreement. It fixed annual Ministerial EU-Troika meetings, and opened the door to a broad political dialogue.

In 1996 the Commission Communication for an "EU-India Enhanced Partnership" was endorsed by the Council and the European Parliament which was a leap forward and contributed to put the Commission in the driver's seat of EU-India relations.

The intensity of dialogue improved and in 1997 the Commission suggested five "mechanisms" for reinforcing political relations. They were agreed with India at the 1997 Luxembourg Ministerial meeting:

1. Senior Officials Meetings;

2. Meetings between Commission and Indian planners;
3. Bilateral meetings in margins of multilateral fora (two meetings on Biological & Toxicological Weapons);
4. Working groups of specialists
5. Think-tank network:

The 1990s witnessed lots of changes internationally as well as in India. Internationally, USSR collapsed thereby ending cold war. This meant that the threat of Communist expansion has become thing of the past. As for India, the New Economic Policy crafted by Dr. Manmohan Singh, the then Finance Minister ushered in the era of liberalism, privatization and globalization in Indian economy. This facilitated the growth of Indian economy thus establishing India economic potential. The series of Nuclear tests conducted by India also confirm its placed among the great powers of the World. The fall of the Soviet Union ushered in a new era in Indo-US relations. All these developments of the early 1990s helped, though not solely responsible for better, closer EU-India relationship.

The India-EU relations took another forward leap in 2000. The year saw a climb moving from Ministerial-EU Troika to Summit-level annual meeting, the single most important milestone in enhancing EU-India relations since 1990. The first ever EU-India Summit was held in Lisbon on 28th June. As such India joined the ranks of five countries, namely the US, Canada, Japan, Russia and China, with whom the EU conducts regular bilateral Summits. The Summit issued a Joint Declaration along with an Agenda for Action. In this Summit it was decided to have Ministerials Meeting yearly, Senior Officials Meetings twice a year, and Summits on a regular basis. Thus set a faster and newer pace for India-EU relations.

For the EU, the Summit represents the long overdue acknowledgement that India is an increasingly significant political and economic player on the global stage, ever since India had been left in the cold after its key ally, the Soviet Union crumbled at the end of the cold war. As a stable, multi-ethnic and multi-religious democracy with a secular state, India provides a very valuable model for handling cultural and religious pluralism. The summit also gives additional impetus to its policy of engaging India on all major issues of interest and concern.

For India the Summit is a welcome opportunity to be recognized as a truly global player, receiving the same attention as other major partners of the EU. Also the EU soft power nature is a positive model for India's own influence in its regional neighbourhood. Not only for India but also for the region as a whole the EU, as an example of regional integration is a relevant model for some of the current efforts aims at reinforcing regional cooperation in South Asia.

Not only this, India and EU, the two largest democracies have their partnership anchored in shared values and belief and mutual respect. Their commitment to freedom, democracy, pluralism, multi-lateralism and rule of law is a factor contributing to global stability and peace. Both pursue economic progress and prosperity for their people in a peaceful, stable and secure global environment. They also share the belief that no one country can single handedly take care of the problems and challenges of fighting terrorism and organized crime, eradicating poverty, tackling climate change, promoting human rights and democratization to reforming the UN, as these problems and challenges require cooperation at the global level on an unprecedented scale. In recent years, the relationship has developed exponentially in terms of share vision, goals and challenges. Against this background the relationship was upgraded from Summit level Ministerial Meetings to that of "Strategic Partnership' in 2004 with the following objectives:

- international cooperation through multi-lateralism, including promoting peace, combating terrorism, non-proliferation and human rights;
- enhance commercial and economic interaction, in particular through sectoral dialogue and dialogue on regulatory and industrial policy;
- cooperation on sustainable development, protecting the environment reducing climate change and combating poverty;
- continuous improvement of mutual understanding and contacts between the EU's and India's civil society.

In addition, the Summit agreed on the following

- the first-ever EU-India Cultural declaration;
- the creation of an India-EU energy panel,
- the launch of a 33 million Erasmus Mundus Window for some 1000 Indian students to receive a scholarship for post-graduate studies in Europe.
- the creation of joint workshops in automotive engineering, genomics and life sciences and nanotechnology
- an EU-India Environment Conference.
- space partnership
- the Galileo programme (the European global satellite navigation system)

The EU-India relationship now covered all sphere of life-political, economic, social, cultural, education, science and technology, and so on. It is not limited to government to government interaction. Interaction is also at people to people level through NGOs, civil societies, exchange of students and researchers, knowledge workers, etc. and in private sectors through institutionalized Business Summits, CEOs Round Table, High Level Trade Group, etc..

With the launching of the EU-India Strategic Partnership, and in the subsequent years that follows, EU-India have made comprehensive Joint Action Plans setting out a road map for India-EU interaction in diverse sectors, review the implementation and progress of the same and also made Press Statements, Declarations on areas identified above. They also joined hand to unequivocally condemn all acts, methods and practices of terrorism and have stressed solidarity and international cooperation as integral to combating terrorism effectively. A free trade agreement which took the bilateral relationship beyond the WTO framework marked another decisive step in the upgrading of relations.

Thus, India-EU relations which started in cordial, but purely economic on bilaterally, slowly and gradually developed into one that of Strategic partnership. Both India and EU has much to gain and learn from each other. Their commitment to intensify the relationship is grounded in both economic as well as socio-political interests. Economically, EU is India's main trading partner, the largest source of FDI and main provider of technology. EU's export to India is ever growing while India has become an important production base and outsourcing for EU operators. EU has much to gain from India's experience as a multi-ethnic, multi-religious secular democratic state, while India can imbibe the idea of soft power from EU.

The common value based ground and mutual belief of freedom, democracy, pluralism, multilateralism and rule of law of India and EU resulted in designing a high profile dialogue program to further the emergence of shared interests and cohesive roles in international relations. It aims to search for answers to crucial questions of bilateral significance including issues of global security, terrorism, regional conflicts and the newly emerging shifts in Asia and the world. The people to people interactions between the two through exchange of students, researchers, cultural programmes, business summits, NGO and civil societies is one of the single most factor in bringing understanding, mutual respect, cooperation and peace beyond government to government and also help in fostering closer and more lasting relationship.

NOTES

1. Robert Barrass and Shobana Madhavan, *European Economic Integration and Sustainable Development: Institutions, Issues and Policies,* (London, 1996) p. 251.
2. D. Lasok, *The Law of Economy in the European Community,* (London, 1980) p. 291-293.
3. *Bulletin of the European Community,* Supplement no.5, 1991, p. 9.
4. *Ibid.*
5. Clive Archer and Fiona Butler, *The European Community: Structure and Process,* (London, 1992) p. 63.
6. David Coleman and Deborah Robert, *Economic of CAP in transition,* in Mike Artis and N.Lee eds, *The Economic of EU: Policy and Analysis,* 2nd ed (Oxford, 1997) p. 102.
7. Barass and Madhavan, *op. cit.,* p. 254.
8. *Ibid.* p. 255.
9. Coleman and Roberts, *op. cit.,* p. 103.
10. *Ibid.* p. 106.
11. Barass and Madhavan, *op. cit.,* p. 256.
12. *Ibid.*
13. Agenda-2000. For a stronger and wider Union, European Commission, *Bulletin of EU,* Supplement no. 5 (Luxembourg, 1997), p. 26.
14. *Ibid.* p. 27.
15. *Ibid.* p. 29.
16. Clive Archer and Fiona Butler, *The EC Structure and Process,* (London, 1992), p. 79.

17. Pinder John, *The European Community: Building of a Union,* (Oxford, 1991), p. 121.
18. Robert Bladen-Hovel, *The European Monetary System,* in Mike Artis and N. Lee eds. *op. cit.,* p. 331.
19. Archer and Butler *op. cit.,* p. 82.
20. *Ibid.*
21. Barrass and Madhavan, *op. cit.,* p. 155.
22. Bladen hovel, *op. cit.,* p. 332.
23. Archer and Butler, *op. cit.,* p. 83.
24. *Ibid.,* pp. 83-84.
25. Barrass and Madhavan, *op. cit.,* p. 158.
26. Mike Artis, *European Monetary Union,* in Artis and Lee eds., *op. cit.,* p. 349.
27. Barrass and Madhavan, *op. cit.,* p. 159.
28. Werner Weidenfeld and Wolfgang Wessel, *Europe from A to Z: Guide to European Integration* (Luxembourg, 1997), p. 72.
29. *Times of India,* 3rd January 1999, "*Launch of Euro Herald New Era of Europe",* (New Delhi).
30. Angola, Antigua, Bahams, Barbados, Belize, Benin, Botswana, Burkina Faso, Burundi, Cameroon, Cape Verde, Central African Republic, Chad, Comoros, Congo, Cote d'Ivoire, Djibouti, Dominica, Dominican Republic, Equatorial Guinea, Eritrea, Ethopia, Fiji, Gabon, The Gambia, Ghana, Grenada, Guinea, Guinea-Bissau, Guyana, Haiti, Jamaica, Kenya, Kiribati, Lesotho, Liberia, Madagascar, Malawi, Mali, Mauritania, Mauritius, Mozambique, Namibia, Niger, Nigeria, Papua New Guinea, Rwanda, St. Kitts and Nevis, St. Lucia, St. Vincent, Sao Tome and Principe, Senegal, Seychelles, Sierra Leone, Solomon Islands, Somalia, Sudan, Suriname, Swaziland, Tanzania, Togo, Tonga, Trinidad and Tobago, Zuvalu, Uganda, Vanvata, Western Samoa, Zaire, Zambia, Zimbabwe.
31. Archer and Butler, *op. cit.,* p. d120.
32. *Ibid.*
33. *Ibid,* p. 121.
34. The title taken by the newly independent African States under Convention.

35. Archer and Butler, *op. cit.*, p.122.
36. Trevor Parfill, *"Decline of Eurofrica? Lome's mid term remains" Review of Political Economy*, vol.23, no.67, March 1996 (Sheffield), p.53
37. Archer and Butler, *op. cit.*, p. 126.
38. *Ibid.*
39. *Ibid.*, pp. 127-128.
40. Parfill, *op. cit.*, p. 57.
41. *Ibid.*, pp. 60-61.
42. Archer and Butler, n.5, p. 159
43. Cairn group consists of 8 largely agricultural-oriented countries which have joined together since 1986 to present common position on GATT farm talk. They are Australia, Argentina, Brazil, Canada, Chile, Colombo, Fuji, Philippines, Thailand and Uruguay.
44. Frank McDonald and Stephen Dearden, eds, *The European Economic Integration*, (London, 1992), p. 137.
45. *Ibid.*
46. *Ibid.*, p. 203.
47. Michael Smith, *"The Devil you Know: US and a Changing Community," International Affairs*, (London 1992), vol. 68, p. 115.
48. Archer and Butler, *op. cit.*, p. 165.
49. McDonald and Dearden, *op. cit.*, p. 205.
50. *Ibid.*
51. Simon Nutall, "Japan and EU: the Reluctant Partners", *Survival* (London), vol. 38, 1996-1997, p. 107.
52. *Ibid.*
53. *Ibid.*, p. 110.
54. *Ibid.*
55. *Ibid.*, p. 108.
56. Article 1 of the Cooperation Agreement 1994, *Official Journal of the European Communities*, No. L 222.

5

RESPONSES TO NEEDS
Within and Outside-II

In the previous chapter we have discussed the various policies adopted by the EU and its adaptation the changing needs in the form of CAP, EMU, Lome Convention and also it relationship with the US, India and Japan. In this chapter we will discussed two policy areas of the EU which came into existence during/in the Maastricht Treaty, namely, Common Foreign and Security Policy (CFSP) and Justice and Home Affairs (JHA), both of which constitute the second and the third pillars of the European Union respectively. One characteristic which distinguishes these two pillars from the first pillar and which represent a major set back on supranationalism is the intergovernmental nature of their objectives and the procedures established to accomplish those objectives. In contrast, the first pillar, the EC, is institutional in character. We will first start with the discussion on the CFSP and then on proceed to the JHA.

5.1 Common Foreign and Security Policy (CFSP)

The Common Foreign and Security Policy (CFSP) is a single worldwide system of cooperation between the Member-States of the EU in international affairs. One of the external relations instruments of the EU, it was established under the Treaty of the European Union with an aim to safeguard fundamental foreign policy interests, in particular, the independence and security of the Union, taking into consideration the possibility of a common defence policy and a common defence, to preserve peace and to consolidate democracy, the rule of the law and human rights.

The idea of political integration has been there ever since the establishment of EEC in the 1950s. However, since the failure of two courageous attempts to establish a European defence policy in 1950s and 1960s, the Pleven plan and the Fouchet plan respectively, the emphasis is on gradual transfer of power. This took the shape of EPC, launched informally in 1970. Since then, two key milestones have led to significant development of the CFSP: the TEU, with the introduction of the Title, the second pillar of the EU, and the Treaty of Amsterdam, with the strengthening of decision-making procedures and instruments.

From 1950-1987: The creation of European Political Cooperation (EPC)

The idea of creating common foreign and security policy is not a new thing for EU. In fact it is as old as the ECSC. The first of its kind was the Pleven plan which aim to create an integrated Europe army under joint command. This took the form of European Defence Community (EDC). But due to the sensitiveness of the issue,[1] the idea could not materialize. After this, another attempt was made at political integration, 'European Political Community', aimed at establishing a federal or confederative structure. The Political Community was to have a very wide power and was, in the long run, to absorb the ECSC and the EDC. However, this also never came to fruition as it was rejected by the French National Assembly in 1954. In the early1960s, a draft proposal for 'ever closer political cooperation, a union of states and common foreign and defence policies' known as Fouchet Plan was produced. However, due to the over ambitious nature of the plan, the negotiations between the Member-States floundered in 1962. For almost forty years of European construction, the very expression "common foreign policy" found no place in the Treaties. The focus was on economic integration, that of creating a common market, a less sensitive and contentious issue. From October 1970 the Member-States of the European Community cooperated and endeavoured to consult one another on major international policy problems. However, this was at intergovernmental level in the context of "European Political Cooperation" and the trust was on cooperation in the field of foreign policy and not a joint foreign policy consisting of a universal coverage and binding upon all the six participating states.[2] The agreement on the EPC was facilitated by the fact that it was a much less coercive method and entailed less coordination than its predecessors. The international backdrop to such development in the field of foreign policy also saw the US deeply embroiled in Vietnam; the Middle East in crisis following the 1967 war; the Soviet invasion of Czechoslovakia; and domestic unrest experienced in the Member-States in 1968.

In 1986, the Single European Act formalized this intergovernmental cooperation without changing its nature or methods of operation. It still remained formally outside the remit of the EC institutions as the 'Treaty Provisions on European Cooperation in the sphere of foreign policy' was not an amendment to either the Treaty of Paris or the Treaties of Rome but mostly a codification of the existing practice acting to confirm and supplement the procedures agreed in the reports of Luxembourg (1970), Copenhagen (1973), London (1981), the Solemn Declaration of European Union (1983) and the practices gradually established among the Member-State.[3] The SEA also established a full-time Secretariat at Brussels with a charge of preparing, implementing and administering the EPC matters.

The Common Foreign and Security Policy

The real change came at Maastricht where, for the first time, Member-States incorporated in the Treaty the objective of a "common foreign policy" and transform EPC into an integral part of the three pillars structure of the Union. The main aim was "to assert EU's identity on the international scene in particular through the implementation of a common and security policy including the eventual framing of common defence policy, which may in time lead to a common defence".[4] Apart from this the Treaty in Article 11 sets out its five main principles:

- To safeguard the common values and fundamental interests of the Union;
- To strengthen the security of the Union;
- To preserve peace and strengthen international security; to promote international cooperation;
- To develop democracy and the rule of law, including human rights.

CFSP constitutes a separate pillar of the EU because the way it operates and its intergovernmental nature distinguish it from the traditional pillars of the Community such as the single market and trade policy. The difference is most striking in the decision-making procedures, which requires Member-State consensus, whereas in the first pillar a majority vote suffices. In addition, the instruments of the CFSP- common positions, joint actions, decisions, the conclusions of international agreements, declarations and contacts with third countries- differ from those of the EC. These instruments are discussed later in this same chapter.

Unlike in the first pillars, the role of EC institutions like the Commission, the Parliament and the Court of Justice are minimal while the Council of Europe and Council of Minister are the main driving force in the EU second pillar

Since the Treaty's entry into force on 1st November 1993, the European Union as such can make its voice heard on the international stage, express its position on armed conflicts, human rights and any other subject linked to the fundamental principles and common values which form the basis of the European Union and which it is committed to defend. This is in sharp contrast to the modest aims of the EPC process and focus on joint foreign policy for the Member-States of EU as well as binding in nature.

The Amsterdam Treaty

The provisions on the CFSP were revised by the Amsterdam Treaty which entered into force in 1999. The Member-States felt for the need of revising the Maastricht Treaty because the joint action of the second pillar did not work as satisfactorily as the might have hoped. To improve the effectiveness and profile of the Union's foreign policy the Treaty added a post of High Representative who is responsible for assisting the Council in CFSP- related matters by contributing to the formulation, preparation, and implementation of decisions. Mr. Javier Solana Madariaga, who took up the post on 18 October 1999 for a period of 5 years, was the first High Representative of the CFSP. His appointment is significant as Mr. Madariaga who is also a Secretary of NATO is a political figure and also represents a shift from over-dependence of Europe on US defence and security.

The Amsterdam Treaty reaffirms the five principles set out in the Maastricht Treaty and also identifies several ways in which these objectives are to be pursued:

- defining the principles and general guidelines for the common foreign and security policy, which is done by the European Council;

- deciding on common strategies. These instruments were introduced by the Amsterdam Treaty and set out overall policy guidelines for activities with individual countries. Each strategy specifies its objectives, its duration and the resources that will have to be provided by the EU and the Member-States. So far there are Common strategies on Russia, Ukraine, Mediterranean and the Middle East Peace Process. They too are decided by the European Council.

- adopting joint actions and common positions. These commit the Member-States to adopting a certain position and a certain course of action. They are decided by the General Affairs Council.

The Amsterdam Treaty also added a new foreign policy instrument to the existing ones, namely the common strategies, to be applied in areas where the Members States have important interests in common. A slight improvement has also been made in regards to decision making. It allows for adoption by qualified majority in two cases- for decisions applying a common strategy defined by European Council and for any decisions implementing a joint action or common position already adopted by the Council.

The Treaty of Nice contains new CFSP provisions. It notably increases the areas, which fall under qualified majority voting, and enhances the role of the Political and Security Committee in crisis management operations. It also established European Security and Defence Policy (ESDP) and set up three instances: a Committee for Civilian Aspects of Crisis Management, a Military Committee and Political-Military Group for enhancing the effectiveness of the crisis management operation.

Structure and Procedures

The EU has no single, permanently unified foreign ministry, or a single network of embassies or permanent diplomats. The development of the inter-governmental framework, described above, has created a structure that is composed of elements drawn from the Member-States, but simultaneously these operate as facilitators and manifestation of the international identity of the EU.

CFSP followed the structure and procedure initiated under the EPC, with omission and commission. Under EPC, ministerial meeting of the Foreign Ministers were held twice a year in the early years which later got increase to four times a year. Convening of the meetings was the sole responsibility of the President in office and held in the country of the President in office. The host State bore the burden of administration and each state was to appoint one of its officials as the 'correspondent' to counterparts in the other participating state. As such the day-to-day control and administration was firmly in the hands of individual government.

The position of the President is not permanent but rotated among the Foreign Ministers in such a way so as to ensure that the same Member-State holds the presidency of the Council of the European Communities at the same time.

The actual or ground work for the meeting of the Foreign Minister was done by "Political Committee" consisting of the heads of the political departments of the Member-States who would meet at least four times a years or as frequently as the intensification of work required. The Political Committee has the power to form 'working parties' for 'special task'.

The interaction between EPC and the institution of EC were minimal as EPC function outside the purview of EC. The Commission was consulted only if the activities of the EC are affected by the work of the Ministers, informal meeting between member of European Parliament, Political Committee and the Foreign Minister held only twice in a year and the President in office give an annual report of EPC to the full Parliament.[5]

The Treaty of European Union incorporated most of the structures and procedures of the EPC albeit some alteration. EPC ministerial meeting was terminated and replaced by the European Council that comprised of the Heads of the State and Government. Instead of discussing issues at ministerial level, which again is review by the concerned Member-States, the issues of CFSP now get discussed by the Heads of the State and Government themselves. The Council is now the sole forum for CFSP. However, the preparation of CFSP items remains the responsibility of the Political Committee. The Political Directors now meet on a monthly basis with the European Correspondent responsible for day-to-day contacts thereby transferring the day-to-day control and administration from the hands of individual government to that of European Union.

The Treaty of Amsterdam as well as the Treaty of Nice added some more changes in the CFSP. As mentioned earlier, the Treaty of Amsterdam added a post of High Representative, a highly decorated and high profile post with lots of importance attached to it. The Treaty of Nice established a new permanent Political and Military structures to provide political control and strategic direction in crisis by setting up a Political and Security Committee. Another changes brought about by the Treaty of Nice were the establishment of a Committee for Civilian aspects of crisis management, a Military Committee and a Political-Military Group. All these are based at Brussels in the Council's building.

Instruments of Implementation

The CFSP uses certain specific instruments. Some are provided for by the Treaty of European Union and some by the subsequent treaties. However, it does not have legal instruments such as the "directives" or "regulations" used for Community policies. They are Consultation, Common Position, Joint Actions, Decision and Conclusion, Common Strategies and Statements.

1. **Consultation Procedures**[6]—In this procedure, the Member-States agreed to inform and consult one another within the Council of Ministers on matters of foreign policy of general interest. This is done so that the combine efforts of the Member-States may be exercised as effectively as possible through concerted and convergent action. This procedure requires information and consultation, but not much else. It is similar to the obligation imposed on the Member-States under the SEA.

2. **Common Position**[7]—One of the means of effecting the CFSP, it is a specific, single and articulated position on a matter of international concern to the Union as well as to the Member-States. Common positions are binding on the Member-States. The Members, then commit themselves to ensure that their national policies conform to the common position and take action necessary to implement the common position. For instance a common position was adopted in the framework of sanction taken against the Federal Republic of Yugoslavia, according to which the EU Member-States' authorities should not grant entry visas to certain Federal Republic of Yugoslavia citizens due to their close connections with the Melosevic regime. The names of these persons are placed on a continually updated list.

   Common positions are as a rule adopted unanimously, except when a common strategy is being implemented. For more effective working, the Member-States agreed that within CFSP, when the Council is to act by unanimity, they would 'to the extent possible' avoid preventing a unanimous vote if a qualified majority favours the decision.[8] Common positions are decided by the General Affairs Council.

3. **Common Action**[9]—The third means of

implementation of CFSP is joint action of the Union. A joint action means a specific action or activity undertaken by the Union in responses to a foreign policy concern. Joint actions are adopted by the Council when the EU wants to take operational action on a specific area of foreign policy. For examples in deploying election monitors, appoint a special representative, impose certain sanction etc. The text of each action should specifies its objectives, scope, the means to be made available to the Union, the conditions for its implementation and, if necessary, its duration. The Council of Minister on the basis of guideline furnished by the European Council decided whether a matter should be the subject of joint action. All three form of voting—qualified majority, quasi-unanimity and unanimity are used in taking joint actions. Which form of voting is adopted for particular matter depends on the Council decision. The initial decision as to whether a joint action should be undertaken requires the same "quasi-unanimity" as the common position.[10] All decision requires unanimity, except those more specific decision, which the Council of Ministers unanimously agrees, shall be made by qualified majority. Once the Council decides upon a joint action, that action stands until modified or terminated by the Council.

4. **Decisions and conclusion of international agreements**—In the context of the CFSP, the Council can also adopt decisions which, like common positions and joint actions, are binding on the Member-States. It also concludes international agreement with one or more states or with international organization in CFSP sphere. In such case the Council authorizes the President to enter into negotiations. The Council, acting unanimously, on the recommendation from the President, then concludes the agreements. Like other

means of implementation conclusions are also binding on the Member-States as long as the conclusions comply with their own constitution.

5. **Declarations and Statements**—the Union additionally makes evaluative statements or declarations on current political topics to give public expression to a position, request or expectation of the EU vis-à-vis a third country or an international issues. This flexible instrument makes it possible to react quickly to sudden incidents in a particular part of the world and to state the Union's point of view. There are two types of declarations. One entitled "Declaration by the EU" where the Council meets and adopts a position on an international issues and the other entitled "Declaration by the Presidency on behalf of the EU" where the Council does not meet.

6. **Common Strategies**—It is a new instrument introduced by the Treaty of Amsterdam and set out overall policy guidelines for activities with individual countries. Each strategy specifies its objectives, its duration and the resources that will have to be provided by the EU and the Member-States. So far there are Common strategies on Russia, Ukraine, Mediterranean and the Middle East Peace Process. The aim was to create a form of EU legal mechanisms, which would tie the policy of decisions of the Member-States more closely than before to a joint EU line and thus contribute to greater coherence in CFSP. Common strategies can contain a comprehensive EU concept on a given area of foreign policy and set out in binding form a range of concrete measures to implement this concept. Common strategy is adopted unanimously by the European Council and common position and Joint actions are the two measures of implementing the strategy.

7. **Contact with third countries**—This take place mainly through 'political dialogue meeting' and 'demarches'. The EU holds a political dialogue with a large number of countries or groups of countries on questions of international policy. Such meetings take place at all levels: head of the States, Minister, Political Directors, senior officials and experts. The EU can be represented by the Presidency, assisted by the High Representative for the CFSP or by the High Representative alone at the request of the Presidency, or by the Troika (President assisted by the High Representative for the CFSP and the Commission and where appropriate, the next Presidency) Demarches, which are confidential, are undertaken *vis-à-vis* third countries by the Presidency or by the Troika on behalf of the EU. The main issues of concern of such contact are mostly relating to human rights, democracy or humanitarian action.

Agents of CFSP

The Common Foreign and Security Policy is not implemented in the same way as Community policies (e.g. the agricultural, environmental, transport and research policies). Although the policy is intergovernmental in nature there are many actors involved in the process. However, in view of the sensitive nature of questions affecting international relations, the Treaty naturally attaches great importance to the Member-States and the bodies of the European Union in which they participate directly, i.e. the Council and its competent instances (committees, working parties).

1. *The European Council*: It occupies the position of highest rank in CFSP in that it determines the policy's principles and general guidelines including those relating to matters with defence implications.

It meets at least twice a year. In the meeting, the Heads of the State or Government of the EU Member-States are accompanied by the Foreign Affairs Ministers and the European Commissioner responsible for external relations. The meeting is held at the country of the Presidency.

2. *The Council of the EU*: It is composed of ministerial representatives of each Member-State. CFSP matters are dealt with by Foreign Ministers in the General Affairs and External Relations Council. The Council has to take the necessary decision concerning the formulation and implementation of the CFSP on the basis of the general guidelines or common strategies laid down by the European Council. To that end it adopts the common position and joint action as well as decisions. It is also responsible for ensuring that the Union's action is unified, consistent and effective.

   The proceedings of the Council are prepared by the Permanent Representatives Committee (COREPER). The Permanent Representatives (Ambassador) act in this area in the same way as for the other Community policies. The Political Committee and the Political and Security Committee which monitor the international situation also contributed to the formulation of policies by giving the Council opinions, either at the latter's request or on their own initiative. At the same time it also oversee the implementation of the policies that are agreed.

3. *The Presidency*: In its capacity as the President of the European Council of the EU, and the subordinate bodies responsible for preparing proceeding such as Coreper, Political Committee/Political and Security Committee and working parties. The Presidency provides the impetus and ensures follow up. It

represents the Union in CFSP matters, notably by conducting political dialogue with third countries on behalf of the Union. It is responsible for the implementation of CFSP decisions. It is on that basis that it expresses the position of the Union in international conferences.

The Presidency is assisted in these tasks by the Secretary-General of the Council/ High Representative for the CFSP, in association with the EC. The Presidency may also be assisted by the Member-States which will hold the following Presidency.

4. *The High Representative of CFSP*: Created under the Treaty of the Amsterdam, the High Representative assists the Council by contributing in particular to the formulation, drawing up and implementation of political decisions and, where necessary, by acting on behalf of the Council at the request of the Presidency and conducting political dialogue with third parties. Mr. Javier Solana Madariaga is the first and present High Representative of the CFSP.

   In his position as the Secretary-General of the Council, the High Representative is in charge of the general Secretariat. He is assisted by a Deputy Secretary-General. Their main tasks are to assist the Presidency, prepare the Council's work at all levels and ensure that it proceeds smoothly.

   The following three are directly under the direct authority of the High Representative—the Policy Planning and Early Warning Unit; the Joint Situation Centre (SITCEN) and the EU Military Staff (EUMS)

a) **The Policy Unit**: Set up by the Amsterdam Treaty, the Policy Unit is staff by diplomats and officials put at the disposal of the Council by the Member-States, the

Commission and the Western European Union and by officials from Council Secretariat. It is organized into six specialist task forces covering regional and horizontal issue. Its main tasks within CFSP as laid down by the Treaty are:

- to monitor and analyze developments and provide timely assessments and early warning of events or situation which may have significant repercussions, including potential political crises

- to provide assessments of the Union's interests and identify areas where the CFSP could focus in future, and to produce argued policy—options papers in as a contribution to policy formulation in the Council.

Apart from these, it also provides direct policy support to the High Representative and its staffs act when necessary as contact points between their seconding Member-States or institutions.

b) **The SITCEN**: Like the Policy Unit, the SITCEN also provides timely assessments and early warning of events or situations which may have significant repercussions for the EU's CFSP. It reports to the High Representative and competent bodies for crisis management. The SITCEN is a round-the-clock operational contact point for the High Representative and close collaborators as well as for similar Situation Centres/Crisis Cells inside and outside EU. Its staffs consist of both military and civil officials.

c) **The EUMS** consists of military experts from Member-States seconded to the General Secretariat of the Council and is attached directly to the High Representative. It is headed by Lieutenant General. The task of EUMS is to provide early warning, situation assessment and strategic planning for crisis management operations, including the identification of national and multi-national European forces, and to implement policies and decisions as directed by the Military Committee it is to assist.

5. *The European Commission*: The involvement of European Commission in the process of CFSP is that of association than an initiator or executive. The Commission is fully associated with the work carried out in the field of CFSP. The Commission may, as any Member-State, refer to the Council any question relating to CFSP and may submit proposals to the Council—although it does not have the sole right to do so as in Community matters. The Commission may also, as any Member-State, request the Presidency to convene an extraordinary Council meeting and make suggestions to the Policy Unit for work to be undertaken. The Commission also implements the CFSP budget (under the EC budget) through appropriate financial proposals. The TEU stipulates that the European Commission is to be fully associated with the work carried out in the CFSP field to ensure the consistency of the CFSP with external economic relations and development cooperation and humanitarian aid, which a Community policies in which the Commission plays a leading role.

   The European Commission is represented by its President in the CFSP. He participates in meetings of the Council and its preparatory bodies and in the political dialogue with third countries. It can also lay before the Council any foreign and security policy issue and submit initiatives to it. However, unlike in the Community policies, the initiative power of the Commission is very limited in the CFSP. The Commission, like the Presidency inform the European Parliament of CFSP development.

6. *The Member-States*: All the Member-States of the EU are bind by the Treaty of Amsterdam to support the CFSP actively and unreservedly in spirit of loyalty and mutual solidarity. They have the right to lay before the Council any CFSP issue and submit proposal to it. They ensure that their national policies conform to the common position and support these common positions in international fora. They undertake to uphold the joint actions and their diplomatic services abroad cooperate to ensure compliance with and the implementation of common positions and joint actions.

The European Security and Defence Policy (ESDP)

Any discussion on CFSP cannot be complete without discussing ESDP. Established under the Treaty of Amsterdam, it covers all matters relating to its security, including the gradual formulation of a common defence policy as well as common defence if the European Council were to decide and decisions were adopted and ratified by the Member-States. However, the ESDP does not affect the specific nature of the security and defence policies of certain Member-States and is also compatible with the policy conducted in the framework of the NATO.

The main objective of ESDP is to develop Union's capacity for autonomous action, backed by credible military forces, the means to decide, to use them, and a readiness to do so, in order to respond to international crisis without prejudice to actions by NATO which was to become operational by 2003. This marks a breakaway of the EU Countries from its traditional dependent on US and NATO for security and defence which has been there since the World War II.

The capacities and structure of ESDP are divided into three components. The first two, military crisis management and civilian crisis management, are known as the Petersberg tasks while the third one is the conflict prevention. Since 1999 crisis management is at the core of the process of strengthening the CFSP. As such conflict prevention has been given priority. The Petersberg tasks operate through.

- Humanitarian and rescue tasks
- Peacekeeping tasks
- Tasks of combat forces in crisis management, including peacemaking.

The Union's consistent overall approach to crisis management is to develop a coherent approach using the whole range of civilian instruments already at its disposal while also being able to use military force.

Military capability: Introduced by Helsinki European Council, and strengthen by Nice European Council. The former one set the headline goal -the Union capability to deploy within 60 days, and sustain for at least one year, up to 6000 troops. The latter strengthen this capability by introducing new military structures, the most important, the Political and Security Committee (PSC). The main task of PSC is to keep track of international developments, help define policies and monitors implementation of agreed policies. In this, the PSC is assisted by a politico-military working group, a committee for civilian aspects of crisis management, as well as the EU Military Committee (EUMC) and the EU Military Staff (EUMS). The EUMC, in turn gives military advice to the PSC and the High Representative while the EUMC, which is a part of the Secretariat of the Council, is responsible for early warning, strategic planning and situation assessment.

Civilian capability: It was developed in the Feira European Councils, 2000 and Gothenburg European Council, 2001. Four areas of cooperation are prioritized.

- *Police cooperation*—Members States should be able to provide 5000 policemen, deploy 1000 of them within 30 days for international mission;

- *Strengthening the rule of law*—Member-States should be able to provide 200 judges, prosecutors and other experts in the field of rule of law;

- *Strengthening civilian administration*—Member-States should be able to provide team to establish or guarantee elections, taxation, education, water provision, etc;

- *Strengthening civilian protection*—possibility of assisting humanitarian actors through emergency operations by having the capability of providing 2 to 3 assessment team, within three to seven hours, consisting of ten experts as well as intervention teams consisting of 200 people.

Conflict Prevention: Developed minimized human suffering and enormous cost generated by violent conflict is the third components of ESDP, the conflict prevention. It aim at ensuring long-term structural stability, seeks to establish/restores a favourable political environment in the region concerned with the goal of promoting peace and stability. Four main objectives of conflict prevention are:

- To make more systematic and coordinated use of the Community's instruments

- To identify and combat causes of conflict

- To improve the capacity to react to nascent conflicts and

- To promote international cooperation in this area

In order to increase the efficiency of conflict prevention, a rapid reaction mechanism was created to provide rapid financing for crisis management. It may be implemented where there is a threat to public order or public safety, or in other similar circumstances that might destabilize a country.

Effectiveness of CFSP

In order to be effective, the CFSP must be consistent with other policies and have an efficient decision-making procedure.

Consistence in the field of CFSP is ensured through keeping the framework, resources, methods and patterns of work for implementing the CFSP within the framework that already existed in the Community's sphere of action. The full association of the Commission in the discussions on the CFSP is one way of strengthening such cooperation. Consistency is also maintained by the European Council by setting out guidelines for the development of the Union, to ensure the consistency of the CFSP with Community policies which are conducted under the responsibility of the Commission.

Decisions in CFSP are generally taken unanimously. This mean that one Member-State can obstruct the proceeding easily. In order to overcome such obstacle, the Treaty includes three options for making the decisions easier. However, unanimity is obligatory for the adoption of decisions with military or defence implication. The three options provided by the Treaty are:

1. *Constructive abstention*: It means abstention by any member when a decision is adopted in order not to block the adoption of the decision. It is done through a formal declaration. In such case the abstained member is not required to apply the decision, it just acknowledge that the decision is binding on the Union.
2. *Qualified majority voting*: The Treaty provided this for smoother and faster decision making in the CFSP. When a decision is taken through this voting, a Member-States may nevertheless invoke important and stated reasons of national policy in order to oppose

the adoption of the text. In such case, the Council may, acting by a qualified majority again, refer to the European Council for unanimous decision. It requires 62 votes in favour cast by at least 10 members out of 15 members.

3. *Enhanced cooperation between several Member-States*: where the objectives of the Union and the Community cannot be achieved by the Member-States as a whole, those Member-States in a position to do so (at least eight Member-States) may establish between them "enhanced" cooperation. In the CFSP field, this cooperation may relate solely to the implementation of a joint action or a common position, to arms initiatives or to security and defence initiatives contributing to the acquisition of crisis management capabilities.

5.2 Justice and Home Affairs (JHA)

The establishment of JHA as the third pillar of the EU by the TEU is an extraordinary phenomenon of the integration process. No other policy making area had make its way as quickly and comprehensively to the center of the treaties and to the top of the EU's policy making agenda as the JHA. At the beginning of the 1990s, JHA did not even exist as policy making area within the scope of the Treaties, and the limited cooperation between the Member-States which has been building up since the mid 1970s took place in range of poorly coordinated intergovernmental groups that lacked adequate institutional structures, legal instruments and objectives. But today, especially, after the Amsterdam reform, the additional impetus given by 1999 Tampere European Council and a broad range of legislation adopted, policy making in JHA has not only become central treaty objective but also one of the most dynamic and expansionist areas of EU development in terms of generating new policy initiatives, institutional structure and its impact on European and national actors.

Justice and Home Affairs have been the fastest growing policy-making area of the EU in the last decade. This is more with the establishment of EU as an "area of freedom, security and justice" (AFSJ) by the Treaty of Amsterdam and in the aftermath of the unprecedented terrorist attacked of 11th September 2001. The areas or subjects that come under JHA are many and varied. They devolve essentially from three fundamental aspects articulated in the concept of the 'area of freedom, security and justice' mentioned above:

- Security, both internal and external aspects. This includes terrorism, crime, drug trafficking, trade in human being, illegal migration etc;
- Justice both civil and criminal; and
- Freedom, in the concrete form of measures on free movement of persons, asylum etc. Freedom is also a basis of governing all JHA activities through implementation of human right.

After a modest beginning of 'third pillar', cooperation in JHA in the first half of the 1990s, JHA have become a core treaty objective and that EU has moved on a massive scale into areas which had for decades, remained an excessive preserve of national sovereignty and action.

Though JHA was established by the Maastricht Treaty, the main objective of establishing and developing the Union "as an area of freedom, security and justice in which the free movement of persons is assured in conjunction with appropriate measures with respect to external border controls, asylum, immigration and the prevention and combating of crime,"[11] was proclaimed by the Treaty of Amsterdam. With this, JHA gained more political importance because it places all other JHA related provisions in the EC and EU treaties under a common rationale, that of creating an "ever closer Union"[12] The Treaties also for the first time identify the EU as a potential provider of internal security for the European citizens. This is explicitly pointed out by both Article 61© TEC and Article 29 TEU which states that EU measures are "aimed at a high level security". With this EU has clearly entered a domain hitherto been the preserve of national state and that too on a massive scale.

The competence area as well as the importance of JHA keeps increasing and, as such, the workload in the field. As many as 40% of the Council's Secretariat General meeting and workload are now directly or indirectly relate to AFSJ matter.[13] Even a special European Council was completely dedicated to JHA policy area in Tampere during the Finnish Presidency. The raising political importance of JHA is also proof by the fact that JHA Council which meets only four times a year has started meeting every month, though only in principle, since December 2001. Such raising importance may be due to the fact that the policy areas of JHA directly related to some of the major concerns of the citizens of the EU: internal security, the combat against drug addiction and organized crime, the problems of immigration, judicial cooperation in civil and criminal matters, etc, which are much closer to the immediate interest of the citizen than, for instance, EMU or CFSP.

Evolution of JHA since the 1950s

Justice and Home Affairs as it exist today is the outcome of many intergovernmental cooperation outside and within the purview of the EU both before and after the Maastricht Treaty. Before the Maastricht Treaty none of the three founding Treaties had given any explicit competences to the Community institutions in JHA. But their introduction as a major policy making areas in the 1990s has clearly benefited from the European cooperation framework outside the EC Treaties. Such cooperation acted not only as mere precursor but also as a sort of laboratories which in many areas experimented with and defined the bases as well as core elements for what then become the EU acquis in JHA.

The European Council

European Council was the earliest inter-governmental organization which addressed the issues relating to JHA in Europe. A major part of Council's activities had been dedicated to the establishment of fundamental element of a Pan-European legal and judicial space. It helps created a number of European conventions which later became the basis for the development of JHA measures within the Union. The European Convention on Extradition (1957) and later additional protocols, the European Convention on Mutual Legal Assistance in Criminal Matters (1959) and the additional protocol of 1978, the European Convention on the International Validity of Criminal Judgement (1970) and the Convention on the Transfer of Sentenced Person (1983) which are also a part of the Union acquis, were agreed upon within the framework of the European Council.

Apart from this, the Council of Europe also acts as space where countries professing different interest learnt how to cooperate and understand each other systemic differences and preferences. The often protracted negotiations on the conventions which were affected by all the substantial difference between the national legal systems provided national administration with the increasing experience in cooperation with the other European countries led to a better understanding of the particular systemic differences and difficulties in partner countries, and gradually created more favourable climate for deeper cooperation in JHA. In a way the Council of Europe led JHA and number of other EU policy-making areas to what the great French lawyer Paul Reuter described as 'the progressive emergence of European mentality'.[14]

However, it was not only the positive points that the EU members learn from the Council of Europe. It also learnt certain negative point from the experience. Due to the larger membership and purely inter-governmental basis of the organisation's proceeding negotiation usually take a long time and in most cases important and ambitious proposals are usually dropped mid-way and if finally agreed upon, contentious points are deleted so as to reach consensus among the members. Such experience made the EU members realize that some of the interest they had in common could not be adequately address within the Council of Europe and provided the incentive for the EC members to move beyond its structural limitations by setting up their own framework and procedures for addressing the JHA issues.

Trevi

This framework went as far back as 1975 and lasted till 1993. It was extremely loose form of inter-governmental cooperation which operated outside the EC framework and as a part of EPC. It functions without any formal treaty provision and has no permanent institution. It has no legal basis and had a very limited mandate, that of fight against terrorism. This acts as a basis on which the EC members gradually develop their cooperation in other areas such as the fight against drug trafficking and organized crime, set up a range of additional working parties and explore more intense mechanism of information exchange and operational cooperation. The inter-governmental working structure of the third pillar in the 1990s was also adopted from the Trevi. Not only this, the Trevi has also played a crucial role for some more substantial elements of progress achieved after the informal introduction of JHA into the EU. One striking example is the establishment of Europol which is as much a product of Trevi cooperation as it is of the EUs third pillar.

Schengen

The Schengen Agreements are an attempt by some of the EU to remove their common border controls and to establish a strong external border, along the lines of the USA.

With its objective of abolishing internal border controls (to facilitate free movement of people) and necessary compensatory measures, it has profound impact on many policy-making areas of JHA. Agreed upon by Germany, France and the Benelux countries in 1985 on intergovernmental basis, the Schengen Agreement deal with visa, immigration, asylum, drug and drug related crime, etc. as such it is seen as pilot project for the integration of JHA in the EU. The asylum policy of EU as it exists today is mostly the outcome of work done in the Schengen. Not only this, the principal criteria for determining the state responsible for examining an application for asylum, the obligations of the responsible state and most of the procedures laid down in the Dublin Convention had been agreed in the Schengen context before consensus was reached in the adhoc Group Immigration which involved all EC Member-States.

One area in which the Schengen had great bearing on JHA is in the matters of visa policy. The uniform visa format of the EU is as much the product of the Schengen as that of the EU. The technical specification provided by the Schengen form the basis on which the Commission was effectively able to steer its proposal through the Council in 1995.

Schengen also has left its mark on judicial cooperation in the EU context. The 1996 EU Convention relating to extradition between the Member-States was at least in part constructed upon and supplemented the provisions on extraditions of the Title III ch.4 of the Convention, Implementing the Schengen Agreement. The emphasis on mutual legal assistance in case of extradition is also more of Schengen approach than the EU.

Another area in which Schengen has left its imprint is in the area of police cooperation. For instance, the drawing up of police/customs agreements in the fight against drugs owes a lot from Schengen experiences. The concept of liaison officers of the EU has also been taken from Schengen system of liaison officers. Apart from determining and facilitating decision making on many matters of EU-JHA, Schengen has also played a more general supporting role. It provide an interesting insight into how the EU members try to reconcile national self-interest with the declared ideals of the Community and Union and served as a fruitful testing ground for exploring both the potential and limits of common ground and specific techniques of negotiation and cooperation. It offered a quicker route to the objective of free internal frontiers than the EU procedures. Both positive as well as negatives experience provided valuable lessons for the EU-JHA, on the extent, limit and the nature of cooperation in the field. It also develops a culture of cooperation amongst the EU Member-States with understanding of the different situations and problems in partner countries.

Driving Factors

Apart from the above three initiatives which facilitated the rapid development in EU-JHA, the development within the EC as well as the international political scenarios also act a driving forces in the process of JHA. The external impetus is provided by the political situation of the time while internal impetus is provided by the development within the EC/EU

External Factors

The emergence of new, or the increase of existing transnational challenges in the areas of justice and home affairs has constantly played a key role in pressurizing the Member-States to agree on intensified cooperation and the build up of new structures at the European level right from the Trevi.

When the Trevi came in being in the 1970s, several Member-States of the EC/EU were faced with the threat of international terrorism, the main factor behind its existence.

As such the main objective of the Trevi was fight against terrorism. The structures and mechanisms of Trevi was further strengthened in the 1980s with the increased realization of the linked between terrorism, organized crime and drug trafficking and changes in international drug-trafficking routes. The introduction of the third pillars of the EU itself was influence by the sharp increased in the number of asylum application and the mounting illegal immigration pressure at the end of the 1980s.

New developments in the field of JHA, sometimes, are triggered off by specific external factors. One glaring example is the introduction of European Refugee Fund after the Kosova crisis. Faced with the problem of large number of refugees and asylum-seekers in spring 1999, the Council adopted a joint action on practical support in relation to the reception and repatriation of refugees, displaced persons and asylum seekers.[15] This joint action facilitate the establishment of a system of burden-sharing within the EU Member-States in cases of major cross-border refugee movements as well as the introduction of a European Refugee Fund in 2000.

Another factor of transnational character that facilitates the development of new policy competence areas in JHA is the challenges arising from technological progress. The rapid growth during the last decade of new forms of crime related to electronic data-processing is an example. Regarding this, the Council has adopted a common position which led the Member to support the inclusion in the Convention on Cyber Crime of the provision facilitating the effective investigation and prosecution of criminal offences against the confidentiality, integrity and availability of computer data, with a particular emphasis also on content-related offences such as child pornography.

Internal Factors

The internal factors stemmed from both the spillover

effects of the Economic Integration as well as the effort to Europeanize certain national problems and the establishment of JHA as an 'area of freedom, security and justice'

The Spillover Effects of the Economic Integration

The completion of internal market has major implication for justice and home affairs. It facilitated the free movement of persons, remove obstacles to cross-border economic activities and necessitate internal security zone encompassing all the Member-States. It also raised a host of questions about measures necessary to compensate for the loss of traditional controlling instruments related to internal border. As such a number of intergovernmental bodies were set up to deal with the issues of police and custom and other issues relating to the abolition of internal border control, asylum, immigration and external border controls and drug trafficking. They later came to be the cornerstones for the development of EU justice and home affairs. The establishment of Europol is one notable example. Without the constraints generated by the internal market programme, the Member-States would not have been willing to go so far with their co-operation on asylum and policing matters at that stage.

The completion of the internal market also facilitates change of perspective and a change of mentality within Europe. All the Member-States as well as other actors of the EU realize that as a result of the rapid progress of economic integration and abolition of internal border, problem of one Member-States such as illegal immigration and organized crimes are directly or indirectly affecting them as well. This created a growing awareness of mutual interdependence and of the need to share information and expand cooperation in this field.

The establishment EU as an 'area of freedom, security and justice' itself is the spillover effects of internal market. It was argued that inspite of the completion of the internal market, both individual and businesses still found it very difficult to gain adequate access to judicial authorities in other Member-States, to obtain judicial decisions within reasonable delays and to have their rights enforced. This became the cornerstone for a rapid development of judicial co-operation. They also gave the Council a mandate to introduce common rules simplified and accelerate cross border litigation on small consumer and commercial claims and common minimum standards for multilingual legal documents used in cross-border cases.[16]

Europeanisation of National Problems

The process of Europeanisation of national problems for common action within the EC/EU also acts as a driving force in development of EU-JHA. The Europeanisation of interests of individual Member-State faced with specific challenges at national level have played a key role in introducing or extending EU action into new JHA areas. Europeanising national problem has twofold benefits:

a) Europeanisation may actually provide a more efficient response to certain problems, especially if these-because of their size or transnational dimension- cannot any longer be tackled effectively by the respective Member-State

b) It can also help by taking the heat off an increasingly acrimonious domestic political debate. Once the issue has effectively been brought to the European agenda, government can try to hide behind the weighty screen of collective EU action.

Following are some examples of such action contributing towards the development and introduction of the EU third pillar.

1. *EU asylum policy*: Between 1990-1991 EC/EU Member-States were facing with the problem of

enormous increased in asylum application. The disproportionate share in the number of application was creating a problem for the German government. In this situation, the German government hoping that a move towards a common European asylum policy would lead to a more even distribution of asylum applications among the Member-States and/or the introduction of a burden-sharing mechanism on one hand. On the other hand, it hope to defuse, to some extent, the increasingly bitter debate about potential restrictive revision of the relatively liberal German legislation on political asylum, that caused of major political polarization in the political landscape and opinion as well as controversies within the ruling coalition. Although the attempted Europeanisation led to only very limited immediate progress towards EU asylum policy-making, it at least partially fulfilled its role in the internal German political debate.

2. *Criminalisation of trafficking in human being and the sexual exploitation of children*: Originally the problem of Belgium, this problem get Europeanised when the Belgium government submitted to the Council a national proposal under article K.3 TEU for joint action regarding a case of abduction, abuse and murder of a child in1996. Known as 'Dutroux affair' the case put into question not only the integrity of Belgium law enforcement authorities but also led to a major political crisis which was threatening to get out of hand. The Belgium government was able to defuse the situation by presenting the problem as European problem by linking the case with a network of paedophiles in neighbouring countries. A joint action was eventually adopted by the Council on 24th February 1997.[17] This became the stepping stone for

further EU measures regarding the criminalisation of Trafficking in human being and sexual exploitation of children including the fight against child pornography on the internet.

3. *Creation of European judicial area*: The French government encountering stiff opposition from large parts of the judicial establishment while trying to proceed with a major reform of the French judiciary presented the difficult national reforms as part of a wider European Project of creating a more open, more efficient and fairer system of justice. With this the French government was hoping to gain more support for the reform at the national level and to increase pressure on the French judiciary to accept it. This had its impact on AFSJ. Although the French approach on harmonization in the judiciary was not follow entirely, emphasis on the progress towards a 'European area of Justice' and the strategic guideline on further action in areas such as access to justice and greater convergence in civil law for EU are the outcome of French effort in the area.

Creation of AFSJ

Although various objectives of JHA were frequently address within and outside the EU system, it was the Treaty of Amsterdam that effectively merged it into the AFSJ as a major new integration project. The Treaty of European Union had made AFSJ as one of the fundamental treaty objectives which itself is a significant step as it places all other JHA related provision in the EC/EU treaties under common rationale. This formally uplift JHA to the same level as economic and monetary and CFSP. Since then, it has been backed up by the detailed Vienna Action Plan of December 1998,[18] partially exceeded by the Tampere European Council Conclusions and supplemented by the new 'scoreboard mechanism'[19]. With it the AFSJ has been launched on a very broad scale.

Big steps have also been taken as regards the build-up of an effective legitimizing political discourse. The Vienna action plan, emphasizes that the new Treaty opens the way to giving freedom 'a new meaning beyond free movement of persons across borders' and that includes the 'freedom to live in a law abiding environment' protected by effective action of public authorities at the national and European level. In line with the TEU objective that the Union shall 'provide citizens with a high level of safety'[20] within the AFSJ, the Tampere Conclusion described the challenge of the Amsterdam Treaty as that of ensuring freedom which includes the right to move freely throughout the Union, enjoyed in condition of security and justice accessible to all. It also added that 'people have the right to expect the Union to address the threat to their freedom and legal rights posed by serious crime.[21]

With this, JHA lost the primarily 'technical appearance' accredited to it after the TEU till the mid 1990s. It is now regarded a major field of political action which comes regularly on the agenda of the Heads of the State and Government, brings national government's to send, in most cases, both the responsible cabinet ministers to JHA Council meeting and occupies prominent places in the Commission's current legislative agenda.

Actors and Instruments of JHA

Justice and Home Affairs uses different instruments and actor, just like the CFSP, in the course of its implementation.

The European Council

The European Council brings together the Heads of State and Government of the Member-States of the European Union as well as the President of the European Commission.

Although its role is not specifically mentioned in the provisions on JHA, it has an important place in this area as for the whole development of the European Union. Meeting at least every six months, this high-level political body instigates the priorities, direction and political guiding principles of the Union. A special European Council devoted exclusively to JHA matters has been organized on 15 and 16 October 1999 in Tampere (Finland).

The Council of the European Union

The Council of the European Union is formed by the representatives of each Member-State at ministerial level. It is generally the Ministers for Justice and the Interior acting within the Justice and Home Affairs Council who deal with justice and home affairs issues. It is for the Council to adopt common positions and framework decisions and draw up conventions, as per the guideline provided by the European Council. Apart from certain exceptions, it acts unanimously.

The proceedings of the Council are prepared by the Permanent Representatives Committee (COREPER). The Permanent Representatives, who are the ambassadors of the Member-States to the Union, act in this area as they do with regard to other Community policies or the common foreign and security policy. They in turn are assisted by the Article 36 Committee (its name derives from Article 36 of the Treaty setting it up) which is composed of senior officials of the Member-States. Its main task is to coordinates activities in the area of police and judicial cooperation in criminal matters and can issue opinions to the Council, either at the latter's request or on its own initiative. Similar ad hoc Committees have been set up to deal with communitarised areas. They prepare the dossiers submitted via Coreper to the Justice and Home Affairs Council.

The Presidency

Every six months, another Member-State of the Union takes it in turn to assume the office of President of the European Council, the Council of the European Union and the bodies responsible for preparing proceedings (COREPER, Article 36 Committee and, at a lower level, working parties). The Presidency plays the role of providing impetus for and following-up proceedings. It is assisted in this task by the General Secretariat of the Council. The Secretariat, which ensures the overall smooth operation of the Council, assists the Presidency, advises it and deals with any organisational difficulties. Directorate-General H deals with three main sectors: asylum/immigration, police/customs cooperation and judicial cooperation in civil and criminal matters.

The Member-States

The Member-States inform and consult one another within the Council in order to coordinate their action and establish cooperation between the various departments of their administrations. They also defend common positions in international fora. But their main role is to provide the initiative: they may propose that the Council adopt common positions or other joint decisions or draw up conventions in all the JHA areas.

The roles of the Commission, the European Parliament and the Court of Justice

The European Commission plays a full part in areas within the framework of the 'third pillar'. However, it does not have sole right of initiative as it does in respect of exclusively Community policies. It shares this role with the Member-States. The Treaty does, however, give it the right of initiative in all JHA areas. Where areas brought under the Community are concerned, the Commission will have sole right of initiative after the transitional period (5 years following the entry into force of the Treaty). The President of the European Commission joins the Heads of State and of Government in the European Council. The Commission takes part in the meetings of the Council, Coreper, the Article 36 Committee and the working parties.

Unlike in the framework of Community policy, the Court of Justice as well as the European Parliament have very limited role in JHA area. In the areas covered by the third pillar, the Parliament must be consulted by the Presidency on all decisions of a binding nature in the JHA area. The Presidency and the Commission regularly inform the European Parliament of the activities undertaken, and the Parliament holds annual discussions on the progress achieved in these areas.

The Court of Justice does not have the authority that it wields in Community policies. As regards the areas that remain within the third pillar (police and judicial cooperation in criminal matters), any Member-State may acknowledge the competence of the Court to give a preliminary ruling on the validity and interpretation of framework decisions and decisions, on the interpretation of conventions and on the validity and interpretation of their implementing measures.

The Court has jurisdiction to review the legality of framework decisions and decisions when proceedings are instituted by a Member-State or by the Commission, e.g. in the case of an infringement of an essential procedural requirement or an infringement of the Treaty. The Court is also competent to settle disputes between Member-States. However, it has no jurisdiction to review the validity and proportionality of operations conducted by the police or other law enforcement agencies of a Member-State or the exercise of the responsibilities incumbent upon Member-States with regard to the maintenance of law and order and the safeguarding of internal security.

JHA Instruments

The JHA uses certain specific instruments. It uses Community instruments such as regulation or directive in the policy area of visa, asylum, immigration and other policies related to external border control, compensatory or flanking measures and free movement of persons as well as judicial cooperation in criminal matters which has been integrated in the Treaty establishing the European Community (TEC or the first pillar). However, with regard to areas remaining within the third pillar, the Treaty provides for the following instruments:

Common positions

The Council of the European Union can adopt "common positions" unanimously. These common positions define the European Union's approach on a given question. For instance, a common position was decided upon, prior to the entry into force of the Treaty of Amsterdam, for the harmonised application of the definition of the term "refugee" in asylum matters. This definition enables national administrations to follow the same guidelines when granting a person refugee status.

Framework decisions and decisions

The Council of the European Union may take framework decisions to approximate the laws and regulations of the Member-States. While these legal instruments are binding on the Member-States as regards the result to be achieved, they remain free to choose the means by which to do so. They are not to entail any direct effect. They are to resemble directive. The Council may also adopt decisions in the JHA area. These decisions does not require any approximation of laws and regulation of the Member-States. They are binding but cannot have direct effect and are supplemented by implementing measures. Prior to 1 May 1999, the Council of the European Union was able to adopt joint actions. For example, it adopted such an action in 1996 to create a directory of specialised competences, skills and expertise to combat terrorism.

The Council adopts framework decisions and decisions by unanimity. Implementing measures, when necessary, may be adopted by qualified majority.

Conventions

Conventions are a traditional instrument of international law. The Council of the European Union may draw up conventions, which it recommends to the Member-States for adoption. Contrary to common positions and other decisions, conventions have to be ratified by all the national parliaments. The implementation of conventions is thus particularly slow and unwieldy.

Since the entry into force of the Treaty of Amsterdam, conventions enter into effect, save as otherwise provided, once they have been adopted by at least half of the Member-States.

Resolutions, Recommendations, Declarations, Conclusions etc.

The Council has resorted to a whole series of instruments to express its political will. It has, for example, adopted a resolution on the protection of witnesses in the fight against organised crime, or a recommendation to prevent disturbances likely to occur at football matches, or even a declaration about motorcycle gangs. These instruments are very often used for their "flexibility": unlike the other instruments mentioned above, they are not binding upon the Council and the Member-State

Effectiveness of JHA

As in CFSP the effectiveness of JHA can be measures from its policy consistency with that of the Community's policy areas and effectiveness of the decision making process.

Consistency

Consistency of JHA is ensured in two ways. Firstly, since cooperation in this field follows from various initiatives regarding police, customs and judicial cooperation which were launched by the Member-States in the 1970s, it work through groups of experts on intergovernmental basis, with no direct link with the EC. The TEU provided a new structure with a permanent secretariat, combined efforts and named the actors and joint instruments for dealing with sensitive issues. Even though some degree of unwieldiness in working structures can be perceived, consistency has largely been improved as a result

Secondly, the consistency of cooperation in the field of JHA can also be viewed in relation to Community policies. This involves the institutions of the EU intervening differently by means of separate instruments such as regulations and directives. To further improve the consistency between the Community policies and JHA, the Amsterdam Treaty transferred asylum, immigration and border control to the Community framework, subject to a few specific adjustments.

Effectiveness of the Decision Making Process

The legal instruments proposed in the CJHA framework have proved difficult to use. No precise description of the effects of a common position or a joint action had been contemplated in the Treaty on European Union. Other tools such as resolutions, decisions and declarations have been introduced. As for conventions, they have proved to be a very unwieldy instrument, as States have to submit them for ratification at national level. Although numerous conventions have been signed, their implementation is still awaited, whereas circumstances often call for rapid responses. The roles of the Commission, European Parliament and Court of Justice, which are weaker than in the Community framework, increased after the Amsterdam Treaty, decision are adopted by unanimity vote.

It should be borne in mind that cooperation in the field of justice and home affairs is relatively recent and new in the context of the Treaty on European Union. It involves national traditions, differing legal systems and administrations which have to find ways of cooperating.

NOTES

1. The reason for failure of EDC has been explain in Chapter 2.
2. Richard G. Whitman, "From Civilian Power to Superpower? The International Identity of the European Union", (London, 1998), p. 76.
3. Ibid. p. 88.
4. Council of the European Communities, Commission of the European Communities, The Treaty on European Union (Luxembourg: Office for Official Publications of the European Communities,1992), pp.7-8.
5. Whitman, *op. cit.,* p.77.
6. Article 12 (1) Treaty of the European Union.
7. Article 15, Treaty of the European Union.
8. Declaration on voting in the field of CFSP, 1992 OJ (c191) 104.
9. Ibid. Article 14.
10. *Vanderbilt Journal of Transnational Law,* p. 881.
11. Article 2, TEU (as amended by the Treaty of Amsterdam) Title I 'Common Provision'.
12. Article 1 TEU.
13. EU-JHA, Sussex European Institute MACES/DICES, Spring 2003 option, p. 2.
14. Paul Reuter, *Organisations Europeenes,* (Press Universitaure de France, Paris, 1965).

15. 1999/290/JHA, Council of the European Union, (Luxembourg: Office for official publication of the EU).
16. *Tampere Conclusions*, Council documents SN200/99.
17. OJL 63, 4.3.1997.
18. OJC 19/1, 23.1.1999.
19. The purpose of scoreboard is to keep under constant review progress made towards implementing measures and meeting the objectives set by the TEU, the action plan and the Tampere Conclusion.
20. Article 29, TEU.
21. Para 6 of Tampere Council.

6

CONCLUSION

In the contemporary era characterized by a marked proclivity towards regional organization to facilitate cooperation in matters of economic, social, politics, etc. the EU is one of the better known among such organizations. It has a profound impact on the European affairs, both at national and individual level, in the past five decades through its approaches to integration as applicable to integration of regional cooperation such as agriculture, commerce, industries monetary, politics, social securities, national security and defense, etc. aspects. The EU today is the most important commercial power in the world with a share of about 21 percent of world trade (19.6 per cent for the US and 10.5 for Japan). It is in fact a highly great achievement coming from countries that were dependent on the US for almost everything, 50 years back. Its relative success is often projected as a role model for other regional organizations.

The emergence of EU as a major regional organization today testify the approach of expansive incrementalism in its evolutionary process. The catalytic factor was the creation of the European Coal and Steel Community (ECSC) in 1952 which binds the coal and steel production of the member countries under common authority outside the control of national governments. The success of the ECSC encouraged the creation of the European Economic Community (EEC) in 1958 to include all the aspects of economy in the integration process. The main emphasis was on the economic integration without involving high politics. This exemplified the functional approach to world peace and cooperation that begins with non-political cooperative arrangement and then eventually enveloping the political/security arena, with the passage of time. As such the EU began its integration process by creating custom union, removal of non-tariff barriers, creation of a single market, single currency, etc. The success in the economic realm prompted the members to extend their policy competence into the political sphere. This found expression in the Maastricht Treaty which introduced two more pillars with the aim of eventual political union and also transformed the EC into the EU.

The issue of enlargement has been a recurring issues in EU's policy and politics virtually ever its inception. The membership enlargement tends to show a tendency of sub-regional grouping till 1995. With few exceptions, the EU members till 1995 are same or equal in development level and from Western Europe. And with the entry of 10 more members from countries Eastern and Central Europe in 2004, the EU is gradually becoming a regional organization. However, since most of these countries' developmental levels are very low, this bring in the necessity of eligibility criteria for membership, which otherwise would affect the process of integration.

One remarkable distinction of the EU is its unique institutional structures, encompassing the Council of Ministers, the European Commission, the European Parliament, the Court of Justice and so on. Created by the ECSC, these institutions were incorporated in the subsequent treaties of EU. Unlike the other regional organisations' institutions, the EU institutions have supranational power, which if exercise have the force of national law. Each institution has specific powers and functions work in harmony for the effectiveness of the EU. Most of the decisions are taken on the basis of majority voting while unanimity is required only when the members feel that their national interests are at stake. This has made the EU more effective than other regional and wider membership organizations, so much so that some protagonists/participants of the on going debate aimed at restructuring of the United Nations are inspired by the structural features of the Union.[1]

The Council of Ministers is the main decision making body of the EU. It consists of the representatives of the all member states authorized to commit the government of that member state. It is dual in nature, that is, both intergovernmental and supranational. But not all members have same votes. However, the votes are weighted in such a way that even the voice of the smallest state is heard. As such there is no complaining of sidelining from any member states unlike other organization having same voting arrangement.

The Commission is the main policy initiator, executive and guardian of the EU treaty. It represents the supranational elements of the Union and is drawn from the member states on the basis of their general competence and independent beyond doubt. It is the main driving force behind the European integration.

The Parliament has no equal in the other regional or international organizations. It is the only directly elected organs of the EU and the largest multinational parliament in the world. The increasing power of the parliament with regard to decision making over time is the indication of the increase of the democratic discourse in the functioning of the EU. A latest instance of the growing influence of the parliament occurred when its activity exposed the unhealthy work practices of the Commissioners, leading finally to resignation of the entire Commission.

A remarkable aspect of the EU's vision is that it is not blindfolded with regionalism, indifferent to outside factors or actors. The EU has shown maturity in dealing with the potential economic competitors (the US, India and Japan) and magnanimity towards the less developed countries recently liberated from colonialism.

As such adjustment has been made on CAP and monetary policy to meet the changing needs within the EU. Various reforms within the CAP marked as shift of emphasis from food sufficiency towards securing environmental friendly production, without which CAP would have become an unnecessary burden on EU budget. The monetary policy of the EU which aims at securing currency stability within Europe was realized on 1st January 1999 with the adoption of single currency 'Euro'. This was possible because of the flexible application of the convergence criteria of membership.

The EU has also been adjusting its relations with non-member states both developing and developed alike. Its institutionalize linkage with developing African, Caribbean and Pacific (ACP) states which took the form of Lome Conventions has been constantly changing. Initially the EU guaranteed the ACP privileged status based on non-reciprocal principle, in the EU transactions. However, the Lome IV, which began in 1990 and run upto 2000, there was marked shift in the equation of the relations. The EU grants and aids were made conditional to sensible economic and social policy, democratic decision-making, observation of basic human rights, etc. There are voices of resentment against this untoward intrusive action. Whether this shift will deeper or damper the EU-ACP relations remains to be seen.

The EU relationship with the US—a giant in the world economy—has not been smooth either. Being a dependent of the US, the US had adopted a benign attitude towards the EU in the beginning. However, this attitude got change over time as the EU trade grows in amount and volume. Some of the EU policies, particularly the CAP has been a major area of the EU-US conflicts. In order to counter the growing economic importance of the EU, the US used the platform of GATT and later on WTO to blunt the effect of the EU policies. It also took a series of unilateral action which change the nature of the World trade. The conflict was not confined to economic realm alone. The US insistence on linking economic with political and security interests was another sources of friction between the two. However, from the 1990s with the end of the cold war, the relationship between the two saw some improvement. This was manifested by the agreement reached on agricultural product at the GATT negotiation and by the involvement of the two in reconstructing the economies and politics of the Central and Eastern European countries.

On the other hand, the EU relation with Japan in the beginning was purely economic and conducted in relative indifference. However, this lack of interest in each other was slowly and gradually abandoned and by the end of the 1980s a full-fledged relations developed between the two. This was facilitated by the changing attitude of the EU members on EU side, while in case of Japan the new muscle the EU acquired through the implementation of the Single Market was the precipitating factor.

Unlike its relation with the US and Japan, EU-India relation has been always cordial from the beginning. From having merely bilateral relation on purely economic areas, EU-India relations climb gradually to Summit level and then finally to that of 'Strategic Partners. The two largest democracies in the world, EU-India have their partnership anchored in shared values and belief and mutual respect. Both are committed to freedom, democracy, pluralism, multilateralism and rule of law. Both pursue economic progress and prosperity for their people in a peaceful, stable and secure global environment. They also share the belief that no one country can single handedly take care of the problems and challenges of fighting terrorism and organized crime, eradicating poverty, tackling climate change, promoting human rights and democratization to reforming the UN, as these problems and challenges require cooperation at the global level on an unprecedented scale. The relationship between India and EU is not limited to government level. It spread down to people level, thereby promoting civil societies interaction, exchange of students and researcher, etc. This help in fostering closer ties between the two.

Also both India and EU has much to learn and gain from their relationship. EU, India's main trading partner, is the largest source of FDI and main provider of technology. EU's export to India is ever growing while India has become an important production base and outsourcing for EU operators. EU has much to gain from India's experience as a multi-ethnic, multi-religious secular democratic state, while India can imbibe the idea of soft power from EU

The Maastricht Treaty was a landmark in the history of EU's evolution. For the first time the Community ventured into an area which has been left out because of it's over sensitiveness—political integration. The establishment of the second pillar, CFSP and the third pillar, JHA is the manifestation of the Member States commitment to go forward in this direction.

The idea for cooperation in the international affairs has been present since the 1950s. However, till 1986 SEA cooperation in the field was at intergovernmental level, outside the framework of the EC. It was the TEU that made CFSP an integral part of the three pillars structure of the Union with an objective of asserting its identity in international scene. The establishment of CFSP heralded a new era in international affairs. From begin dependent on US, especially for security and defense, Europe asserts it independence as well as its intention to be a real actor in international affairs. It no longer remains a mere follower of US or US led NATO policy. This is clearly manifested by the creation of Common Security and Defence Policy (ESDP) that covers all matters relating to its security, including the gradual formulation of a common defence policy. ESDP is backed by credible military forces, the means to decide to use them, and a readiness to do so, in order to respond to international crisis without prejudice to actions by NATO but on line with the UN guideline.

Unlike the second pillar, the development of JHA, the third pillar, as a policy competence area is an extraordinary phenomena in EU's integration process. Before the Maastricht, JHA did not even exist as policy area. However, since its introduction in the Maastricht, policy making in JHA has not only become central treaty objective but also one of the most dynamic and expansionist areas of EU development in terms of generating new policy initiatives, institutional structure and its impact on European and national actors. The reasons for such development are numerous. Some of the policy areas of JHA such as internal security, the combat against drug addiction and organized crime, the problems of immigration, judicial cooperation in civil and criminal matters etc, are the direct concern of the citizen of the EU and are much closer to their immediate interest. Other then these external exigencies such as the September 11 attack on WTC, also contributed much to the faster development of JHA.

The establishment of JHA compliments the Single European Market. It facilitated and expedited the free movement of people enjoyed in condition of security and justice accessible to all. By encompassing policy areas that are traditionally been the sole domain of the national government, JHA like the CSFP, is the physical expression of the EU Member States willingness to move towards united Europe. The establishment of EU as an area of freedom, security and justice is the most glaring example of such an intention.

However, unlike those of the first pillar, the second and third pillars are basically intergovernmental in nature. They both evolved from international cooperations which were mostly outside the purview of the EC/EU. As such cooperations in these two pillars are intergovernmental in character. Instead of the European Commission and the European Parliament spearheading the EU as in the first pillar, it is the European Council that spearheads CSFP and JHA policy areas. The Member States are given more weightage than the EU institution.

Regarding decision making also it differed from that of the first pillars. In the first pillars decisions are taken on the basis of majority voting while unanimity is required only when the members feel that their national interest are at stake but in the second and third pillars it is just the opposite. Since most of the issues in these two pillars constituted a sensitive area for the national governments, decisions are generally taken unanimously. Any one Member State can obstruct the proceeding easily in such type of decision making, as such three options - constructive abstention qualified majority voting and enhanced cooperation – are provided for by the Treaty to overcome such obstacles.

These two characteristics of the second and third pillar undermined the institutional character of the first pillar and put brake to supranationalism. However, it is still very early to draw any conclusion on this basis, as there is increasing involvement of EU institutions like the Commission and Parliament albeit gradually and there is a provision for replacing unanimous decision making by majority voting system from 2004 in the EU Treaty. The probable reasons for preference of intergovernmental characters over supranationalism in the initial years of the second and third pillars existence may be because of its sensitivity of the issues concern. Having experience repeated failure especially in the area of common defense and security the EU Member States took cautious and steady steps so as not to repeat the same mistake over again.

The EU which has achieved so much in the past five decades has many lessons to offer to other regional organizations like SAARC.

The EU in its initial inception concentrated on the economic integration and did not allow the political differences amongst them to hamper the integration process. This is a valuable lesson for SAARC which is marked by regional political differences especially between India and Pakistan.

The institutional structure of the EU is another significant area from which the other regional organizations can learn much about cooperation. Its institutions are supranational bodies which most readily lend themselves to accommodation on the basis of upgrading phases and most likely to develop cumulative decision making precedents. The creation of the Single European Market and the Single European Currency can also encourage the other regional organizations to work towards this direction.

NOTES

1. For details on this debate see Erskine Childers and Brian Urquahart, *Renewing the UN System,* (Dag Hammarskjold Foundation, Uppala, Sweden 1994)

BIBLIOGRAPHY

Primary Sources

Bieber, Roland; Jacques, Jean-Paul and Weiler, JosephH.H ed, *An ever closer Union: A Critical Analysis of the Draft Treaty Establishing the European Union,* (Luxembourg, 1985).

Borchadt, Dr.Klaus-Dieter *European Integration: Origin and Growth of the EU* (Luxembourg), 1995, p.18.

Bulletins of the European Community, (Luxembourg).

Commission of European Communities, The development and future of the Common Agricultural Policy, *Bulletin of the European Communities*, Supplement 5/11, (Luxembourg, 1992).

Commission of European Communities, The development and future of CAP, *Bulletin of the European Communities*, Supplement 5/91 (Luxembourg, 1992).

Commission of European Communities, *The Council of the European Community: An introduction to its structure and its activities* [prepared by Prerre Sabsouls], (Luxembourg, 1991).

Commission of European Communities, *Political Union* (Luxembourg, 1990).

Commission of European Communities, *Single European Act, text, treaties establishing the European Community*, Brussels, 1987.

Commission of European Communities, *European Unification* 1987 (Luxembourg, 1988)

Commission of European Communities, *European Unification*, the origin and growth of the European Community prepared by Dr. Klaus-Dieter Borchadt, Luxembourg, 1995.

Commission of European Communities, Treaties establishing the European Communities (Luxembourg, 1987).

Cooperation Agreement 1994, *Official Journal of the European Communities*, No. L 222.

Council Guide, vol I (Luxembourg, 1997).

European Commission, Agenda 2000 – For a stronger and wider Union, Bulletin of the European Union, Supplement 5/97 (Luxembourg, 1998).

European Commission, Agenda 2000-Enlargement, Bulletin of European of Union, Supplement 4/98 (Luxembourg, 1999).

European Commission, Serving the European Union: A citizen's guide to the institutions of the European Union (Luxembourg, 1996).

European Commission, Europe from A-Z: A guide to European integration by Weidenfeld Werner and Wessel Wolfgang (Luxembourg, 1997).

European Union, Treaty of Nice: Amending the Treaty of EU, the Treaties Establishing the European Communities and Certain Related Acts (Luxembourg, 2001).

European Convention, The European Parliament's Secretariat, Conv 69/02, (Brussels,31 May 2002 (03.06).

Groeban, Han Von der, *The European Community: The Formative Years, the Struggle to Establish the Common Market and Political Union 1958-66*, (Luxembourg, 1987).

Secondary Sources

Books

Archer, C. and Butler, F. *The European Community: Structure and Process,* (London: Publishers, 1992).

Artis, M.J. and Lee, N.eds. *The Economics of European Union: Policy and Analysis,* Second Edition. (Oxford: Oxford University Press, 1997).

Barrass, Robert and Madhavan, Shobhana. *European Economic Integration and Sustainable Development: Institutions, Issues and Policies,* (London: Mc Graw-Hill Book Company, 1996).

Board, Joseph B.Jr *The Government and Politics of Sweden,* (Boston: Houghton Miffin Company, 1970).

Bright, Christopher, *The European Union: Understanding the Brussels Process, the Essential Facts,* (Chichester: John Wiley and Sons, 1995).

Burgess, Micheal, *Federation and European Union: Political Ideas, Influence and Strategies in European Community,* 1972-1987 (London: Routledge, 1989).

Chopra, H.S, *De Gaulle and European Unity,* (New Delhi: Abhinav, 1979).

Cini, Micheal, *The European Commission: Leadership, Organisation and Culture in the EU Administration,* (Manchester and New York: Manchester University Press, 1997).

Claude, Inis, *Swords into Ploughshare: The Problems and Progress of International Organisation.* Fourth Editions. (New York: Random House, Inc., 1970).

Combes, David, *Politics and Bureaucracy in the European Community,* (London: Allen and Unwin, 1970).

Corbett, Richard, *The Treaty of Maastricht: From Conception to Ratification,* (London: Longman, 1993).

Davidson, Nicol, *Regionalism and New International Economic Order,* (New York: Pergamon Press, 1981).

Edwards, Geoffrey and Spence, David. Eds. *The European Commission,* (UK: Cartermill International Limited, 1994).

Fawcett, Louise and Hurrell, Andrew. Eds. *Regionalism in World Politics: Regional Organization and World Order,* (Oxford: Oxford University Press, 1995).

Gallager, Tom *Portugal: A 20th Century Interpretation,* (Manchester: Manchester University Press, 1983).

Gamble, Andrew and Payne, Anthony. Eds., *Regionalism and World Order,* (London: Macmillan, 1996).

George, Stephen *Politics and Policy in European Community,* Second Edition (Oxford: Oxford University Press, 1992).

Gladwyn, Lord, *Europe after De Gaulle,* (New York: Taplinger Publisher Company, 1969).

Goodman, S.F., *The European Union,* Third Edition (London: Macmillan, 1996).

Gowan, Peter and Anderson Perry eds., *The Question of Europe,* (London: Verso, 1997).

Grant, A.J and Temperley, Harold *Europe in the 19th and 20th Centuries:1789-19500,* (London: Longman, 1952).

Grilli, Enzo. R, *European Community and the Developing Countries,* (Cambridge: University Press, 1993).

Groom, A.J.R and Taylor, Paul. Eds., *International Organisation: A Conceptual Approach,* (London: Frances Printer, 1978).

Haas, E.B, *The Uniting of Europe*, Second Edition (Stanford: Standford University Press, 1968).

Hass, E.B, *Beyond the Nation State,* (Stanford: Stanford University Press, 1964).

Hallstein, Walter, *Europe in the Making,* [Translated by Roetler, Charles] (London: George Allen and Unwin Ltd., 1972).

Hayes-Renshaw, Fiona and Wallace, Helen The Council of Ministers (London: Macmillan Press Ltd, 1997).

Henig, Stanley, *The Uniting of Europe: From Discord to Concord,* (London: Routledge, 1997).

Herman, Valentina and Lodge, Juliet, *The European Parliament and the European Community,* (London: Macmillan, 1978).

Holland, Martin, *European Community Integration,* (London: Printer Publisher, 1993).

Huggett, Frank. E, *The Modern Netherlands,* (New York: Praeger Publishers, 1972).

Jacob, Francis and Corbett, Richard, *The European Parliament,* (UK: Longman Group UK Ltd., 1990).

Jain, R.K. *India and the EU in the 21st Century,* (New Delhi: Radiant Publications, 2002).

Jain, R.K,. ed., *India and EU: Building Strategic Partnership,* (New Delhi: Radiant Publications, 2007).

Joll, James, *Europe Since 1870,* Forth Edition (Harmondsworth: Penguin, 1990).

Jones, W. Glyn, *Denmark,* (London: Ernest Benn Ltd, 1970).

Jovanovic, Miroslav. N, *European Economic Integration: Limits and Prospects,* (London: Routledge, 1997).

Lall, K.B., Ernst, Wolfgang and Chopra, H.S. eds., *The EEC in the Global System,* (New Delhi: Allied Publishers Pvt. Ltd. 1984).

Lall, K.B, Chopra, H.S and Meyer, Thomas eds., *European Union and Transformation of Europe's Economy,* (New Delhi: Radiant Publications, 1993).

Lodge, Juliet. ed., *The European Community and the Challenge of the Future,* (London: Printer Publisher, 1989).

Lodge, Juliet. ed., *Institutions and Policies of European Community,* (London: Frances Pinter Publisher, 1983).

Lasok, D, *The Law of the Economy of the European Communities,* (London: Butterworths, 1980).

Lyon, Margot *Belgium* (New York: Walker and Company, 1971).

Mackay, R.W.G, *Towards a United States of Europe,* (London: Hutchinson, 1969).

Mc Allister, Richard *From European Community to European Union: A Historical and Political Survey,* (London: Routledge, 1997).

McDonald, Frank *European Economic Integration,* (London: Longman, 1992).

Miall, Hugh *Shaping the New Europe,* (London: Pinter Publishers,1993).

Minford, Patrick ed., *The Cost of Europe,* (Manchester: Manchester University Press, 1992).

Musulin, Stella *Austria: People and Landscape,* (London: Faber and Faber Ltd, 1971).

Nugent, Neill, *The Government and Politics of the European Union,* (London: Macmillan Press Limited, 1995).

Nye, Joseph *Peace in Paris,* (Boston: Little Brown and Company, 1971).

Pinder, John *European Community: The Building of a Union,* (Oxford: Oxford University Press, 1991).

Roney, Alex *The European Community fact book,* Third Edition (London: Kogan Page, 1993).

Rudden, Dernard and Wyatt, Derrick. Eds., *Basic Community Law,* Fourth Edition (Oxford: Clarendon Press, 1993).

Shaw, Jo, *Law of European Union,* Second Edition (London: Macmillan, 1996).

Slomp, Hans, *European Politics into the 21st Century: Integration and Division,* (London: Praeger, 2000).

Smith, Hazel EU, *Foreign Policy and Central America,* (London: Macmillan Press Ltd, 1995).

Stadler, Karl R., *Austria,* (London: Ernest Benn Ltd, 1971).

Stoessinger, John, *The Might of the Nation,* (New York: Random House, 1969).

Wallace, William. ed., *The Dynamics of European Integration,* (London: Printer Publisher, 1990).

Westlake, Martin, *A modern guide to the European Parliament,* (London, Publishers 1994).

Whitman, Richard G., *From Civilian Power to Superpower? The International Identity of the European Union,* (London: Macmillan Press Ltd, 1998).

Winstrich, Ernst, *After 1992: the United States of Europe,* (London: Routledge, 1989).

Wuorinen, John H, *Scandinavia,* (New Jersey: Prentice-Hall, Inc, 1965).

Articles

Corbett, Richard, "Testing the New Procedures: The European Parliament's first experience with its new 'Single Act' power", *Journal of Common Market Studies,* (Oxford), vol. 27, no. 4, June 1989, pp. 359-372.

Crawford, Gorder, "Wither Lome?: The mid-term review and decline of partnership", *Journal of Modern African Studies,* (Cambridge), vol.34, no.3, September 1996, pp. 503-518.

European Union and the changing European order", *Journal of Common Market Studies* (Oxford), vol.34, no.1, March 1996, pp. 5-132.

Friis, Lyke, "Then they were fifteen: The European's EFTA enlargement negotiation", *Cooperation and Conflict,* (Stockholm), vol.33, no.1, March 1998, pp. 81-107.

Katzenstein, Pete. J., "Regionalism in comparative perspectives", *Cooperation and Conflict,* (Stockholm), vol.31, 1996, p. 126.

Lingnau, Hildengard "Future of Lome Cooperation within the framework of the Development Cooperation of EU," *Economics,* (Metzingin), no.53, 1996, pp. 31-44.

Lodge, Juliet, "The Single European Act: towards a New Euro-synamism", *Journal of Common Market Studies,* (Oxford), vol.24, no.3, March 1986, pp. 203-223.

Masala, Carlo "Institution reform of the EU under debate", *Aussen Politik,* (Hamburg), vol. 48, no.3, 1997, pp. 228-236.

Miles, Lee and Redmond, John "Enlarging the EU: Erosion of Federalism", *Cooperation and Conflict,* (Stockholm), September 1996, pp. 285-310.

Newmann, Manfred. J.M "Reforming the European Monetary System", *Intereconomics,* (Hamburg), vol.29, 1994, pp. 55-58.

Nutall, Simon, "Japan and the European Union: Reluctant Partners", *Survival,* (London), vol.38, no.2, Summer 1996, pp. 104-120.

Parfill, Trevor, "The Decline of Eurafrica? Lome's Mid-term Review", *Review of African Political Economy,* (London), no.67, pp. 53-66.

Pedersen, Thomas, "Problems of Enlargement: Political Integration in Pan-European EC" *Cooperation and Conflicts,* (Stockholm), vol.25, 1990, pp. 83-98.

Pinder, John, "European Community and Nation States: Case of Neo-Federalism", *International Affairs,* (London), vol.62, no.1 Winter 1985.

Preston, Christopher, "Obstacle to EU Enlargement: The Classical Community Method and the Prospects for a wider Europe", *Journal of Common Market Studies,* (Oxford), vol.33, no3, September 1995, pp. 450-463.

Riechel, Andrea Renee, "Japan in the EC: Changing Strategy for Changing times", *Vanderbilt Journal of Transnational Law,* (Tennessee), vol.25, no.1, 1992, pp. 97-136.

Rose, Richard and Haerpfer, Christian, "Democracy and Enlarging the European Union Eastwards", *Journal of Common Market Studies,* (Oxford), vol.33, no.3, September 1995, pp. 427-449.

Serfaty, Simon, "All in the family: the US and Europe", *Current History,* (Philadelphia), vol.93, no.586, November 1994, pp. 353-357.

Smith, Micheal, "The Devil you know: the US and the changing European Community" *International Affair,* (London), vol.68, 1992, pp. 103-120.

Weidenfeld, Werner, "The Single European Act", *Aussen Politik,* (Hamburg), vol.37, no.4, 1986, pp. 378-387.

Index

S

❑❑❑